# READ THIS BOOK
# BEFORE YOUR CHILD
# STARTS SCHOOL

# READ THIS BOOK BEFORE YOUR CHILD STARTS SCHOOL

*By*

**MIRIAM W. LUKKEN**

**CHARLES C THOMAS** • **PUBLISHER**
*Springfield • Illinois • U.S.A.*

*Published and Distributed Throughout the World by*

CHARLES C THOMAS • PUBLISHER
2600 South First Street
Springfield, Illinois 62794-9265

© *1994 by* CHARLES C THOMAS • PUBLISHER

ISBN 0-398-05916-0

Library of Congress Catalog Card Number: 94-14649

With THOMAS BOOKS *careful attention is given to all details of manufacturing
and design. It is the Publisher's desire to present books that are satisfactory as to
their physical qualities and artistic possibilities and appropriate for their particular
use.* THOMAS BOOKS *will be true to those laws of quality that assure a good
name and good will.*

*Printed in the United States of America*
*SC-R-3*

**Library of Congress Cataloging-in-Publication Data**

Lukken, Miriam W.
    Read this book before your child starts school / by Miriam W.
Lukken.
        p.      cm.
    Includes bibliographical references and index.
    ISBN 0-398-05916-0
    1. Reading (Preschool)    2. Reading—Parent participation.
I. Title.
LB1140.5.R4L85      1994
372.4—dc20                                                    94-14649
                                                                CIP

*This book is dedicated to my mother,
Ruth Randolph Willingham, who serves as a living
example of 1 Corinthians 13:4–7.*

# ACKNOWLEDGMENTS

To my husband Peter John for his support and encouragement.

To Ruth Willingham for assistance in typing and obtaining copyright permissions.

To Laura Griffin for her support and help in proofreading this manuscript.

To Marianne Willingham for invaluable advice and sustenance.

To illustrator Suni Harman for the lettering and illustrations that appear in this book.

To teachers Emily Morton, and Maria Willey for their assistance.

To Linda Holt Smith for her computer expertise.

To Judy Stark and Patrick Steel of the U.S. Department of Education.

To my publisher Payne Thomas, and editor, Michael Thomas.

To my daughter Elizabeth for being a guinea pig for the ideas presented in this book.

To these and all quoted in this book I extend grateful thanks.

# INTRODUCTION

Tanya Johnson is an average five-year-old living in the United States today. She spends 42 hours a week watching television. Last week her mother spent less than 15 minutes engaging her in interactive experiences that would expand her mind. This fall, she will be one of the nearly 7 million children who begin kindergarten or first grade. Chances are she will grow up to be one of the more than 36 million Americans who read below an eighth grade level.

Tanya is not prepared for school simply because her parents were not aware of the crucial role they could play in her development.

*Readiness for school is the sole responsibility of the parent.* All children know how to learn, the key is to nurture that instinct in the early years by caring for a child's health and nutritional needs, providing a safe and loving environment, and by helping to develop a child's communication and language skills through stimulating and encouraging a child's natural curiosity.

The first eight years of a child's life are the most important in terms of development. Fifty percent of the development of intelligence takes place before a child enters school, between conception and age 4, and about 30 percent takes place between the ages of 4 and 8. Personality is established, language is learned, attitudes are formed, and intelligence is enhanced or lessened according to the environment of the child.

When a child begins school, the system assumes that the child possesses a certain amount of "shared information" or general knowledge, a starting point, if you will. *Read This Book Before Your Child Starts School* explains to parents, step-by-step, in simple terms, how to get their child to that starting point for a successful school experience, without flash cards, drills, or "forced learning." You can teach a child a lesson for a day, but if you can teach her to learn by creating curiosity, she will continue the learning process as long as she lives.

This book is meant to be a parent's comprehensive guide to ensuring a successful start for their children's academic future. It includes everything parents should know about their child's preschool development and explains what to look for in a school, and its curriculum. The appendix in the back of the book includes a wealth of information to support parents.

By reading this book, you are not only empowering yourself with the knowledge necessary to ensure your child is getting an adequate education, but more importantly, you are giving your child one of the greatest gifts a parent can give a child, a love and respect for learning.

MIRIAM W. LUKKEN

# CONTENTS

## SECTION III   AT SCHOOL

## APPENDICES

# READ THIS BOOK
# BEFORE YOUR CHILD
# STARTS SCHOOL

# SECTION I
# CHILD DEVELOPMENT 101

*Life affords no greater responsibility, no greater privilege, than the raising of the next generation.*

C. Everett Koop, M.D.

# Chapter 1

# THE STAGES OF DEVELOPMENT

In this country you have to have a license to drive a car, catch a fish, or own a business, but absolutely anyone at all can have a child with no training or prior experience. No knowledge, age, or sensitivity are required. This explains many of the problems we face today.

A responsible parent should possess a basic knowledge of child development in order to gain a better understanding of the various stages of his or her child's growth. A parent who knows that it is common for a 4 year old to try out profanity or a six year old to reverse his letters when writing is less likely to react inappropriately when faced with these situations. With this knowledge, you are better equipped to handle the most difficult job in the world—that of a parent.

## THE STAGES OF DEVELOPMENT

The subject of child development includes the physical, psychological, and social growth of the normal child from birth to adolescence.

Generally, childhood is divided into several separate stages, usually on the basis of age. In progressing to maturity, all healthy children pass through these stages which are marked by characteristic changes in growth and development.

### Stages of Childhood

THE NEWBORN CHILD Birth to 1 month
INFANCY 1 month to 18 months
TODDLER 18 months to 3 years
PRESCHOOL PERIOD 3 to 6 years
SCHOOL–AGE PERIOD 6 to 10 years for girls, 6 to 12 years for boys

Studies of child growth and development indicate that each of the stages of childhood has specific characteristics. However, because each stage merges with the following one, the characteristics of a particular

5

stage are most obvious during the middle of the time period. For example, a child of one month still has many characteristics of the former newborn stage, but at the same time is gradually acquiring the characteristics of the infant stage. Similarly, toward the end of infancy a child begins to develop some of the characteristics of the toddler stage. Although all children follow the general pattern of human growth, each child does so in his own unique way.

A child's psychological growth depends on the child's environment. Environment consists of everything with which a child comes in regular or frequent contact, including other people. The majority of children receive the environmental help they need for normal psychological development.

However, psychological growth is also affected by physical factors. For example, advantages in learning ability are influenced by the development of the nervous system. Children do not develop physically at the same rate. As a result, their readiness for psychological growth also varies. A child who develops at a somewhat slower rate than average is not necessarily abnormal.

## The Toddler Stage

The toddler stage lasts from about 18 months to 3 years of age. A child's physical growth is generally slower during this second 18 months after birth than it was during the first 18 months.

By 18 months of age, most children can feed themselves, walk, run a short distance, stack a few blocks, and say a few meaningful words. A toddler is expected to improve all of these skills. But the development of language skills—especially the building of sentences—is a major challenge. Most 2 year olds use one or two words for an entire thought. Parents cannot always be sure what the words mean. For example, a child who says "milk" or "milk gone" may mean anything from "I want some milk" to "I just spilled my milk." By 3 years of age, however, most children can link several words together to form a fairly complete sentence. They can speak about 900 words—an enormous increase over the average 10 to 20 word vocabulary they have at 18 months of age.

Toddlers also vastly improve their powers of imitation and imagination. They may imitate the sounds animals make or pretend an empty cup is a cup of coffee.

A toddler's social relationships develop slowly. Until children are about 2 years old, they tend to be shy around other youngsters. Children usually overcome this shyness after a few minutes, though they may still consider another child more as an object than as a person. By 3 years of age, children start to realize that they have things in common with other children, and begin to regard them as equals.

Toddlers form their strongest attachments to their parents or substitute parents. In most cases the mother is especially looked to for help, comfort, and companionship. The majority of children in Western societies have fewer contacts with the father, though they respect and imitate him. Above all, toddlers want to feel that they have their parents' acceptance and approval. As a result, they are sensitive to any sign of rejection or disapproval.

## The Preschool Years

The preschool years extend from about 3 to 6 years of age. This period helps children prepare for the degree of independence and responsibility they will be given during the next stage of childhood, the early school years. Preschoolers are highly active and constantly exploring the world around them. At the same time, they are beginning to learn that there are certain standards of behavior—things they should and should not do.

By about 3 or 4 years of age, the majority of children have become increasingly aware of themselves and of other people. They are not only more conscious of their own actions, but they have also begun to realize that other people have feelings like their own. Children then start to govern their actions according to the pleasure or displeasure they give another person.

One of the first standards that all children are expected to learn is the process of toilet training. The age when such control becomes possible varies greatly among children, but most children have started to develop it by their third year.

Other standards of behavior include obedience, truthfulness, respect for property, and various sex role standards—that is, the roles that people are expected to play as males and females.

Most parents use rewards and punishments to teach their children standards of behavior. Gradually a child learns that some actions are good and some are bad. In most cases, it is the parent who must decide the goodness or the badness of an action.

Preschoolers also learn standards through a more or less unconscious process called *identification*. The process often begins during the toddler stage, but it becomes fully developed during the preschool years. Children *identify* with another person if they feel they have the same physical and psychological characteristics as that person. Most children identify with their parents or a member of the family.

The majority of 3 and 4 year olds do not know they have a choice in their actions. If something they do displeases their parents, they feel anxious, ashamed, or sorry. But they do not blame themselves for the action. By about 5 years of age, however, most children start to realize that they can choose one action rather than another. Children then begin to feel guilt, as well as shame, if they behave wrongly.

## The Early School Years

The early school years last from about age 5 to 8, and mark a major turning point in a child's psychological development. Children continue to improve their physical skills during this stage. But the period is distinguished mainly by important advances in a child's mental, emotional, and social development.

In most societies, children have been taught basic standards of social behavior by their fifth year. They are also learning to judge whether particular actions are right or wrong. A child can thus be given more independence. However, adults channel this independence along definite lines. In the United States and most other developed countries, children must start school at about 5 or 6 years of age.

Every schoolchild is expected to learn to solve problems, a skill that improves with practice. A 5 year old may try to solve a problem by choosing the first solution that comes to mind. But a 6 or 7 year old thinks about other possible solutions and recognizes why one is better than another. Children this age also begin to see how things are alike and how they differ. Finally, children gain confidence in their mental powers and start to enjoy solving problems correctly.

By the age of 7 or 8, most children begin to rationalize their beliefs— that is, to find reasons for holding them. They may thus decide that the standards of behavior they have learned are good standards to hold. Children this age also increasingly compare themselves with their peers. Such comparisons contribute to a child's *self-image*, the opinion he has of himself. The self-image formed during childhood can influence a person's behavior throughout life.

Children begin to form a self-image during the preschool years as they identify with their parents or other family members. A child's self-image is favorable, or unfavorable, depending on the attitudes and emotions of the person with whom the child identifies. For example, children who see mainly negative qualities in their parents will likely view themselves in a negative light. Children form a more favorable self-image if they have a better impression of their parents. When children compare themselves with other children, they reinforce or alter their basic self-image.

## BEHAVIORAL DEVELOPMENT

What a child can do at any age depends on three main things:

- the opportunities and teachings he receives
- his own individual endowment
- his stage of development

Yet scientists have found that there are definite patterns of behavioral development in studying children. This pattern shows that not only do ages of equilibrium, or stability and balance alternate with ages of disequilibrium, and outgoing ages with inward ages, but that in the years from 2 to 5 one can observe a definite and rather elaborate pattern of behavior change. Interestingly enough, this identical pattern recurs again from 5 to 10 and once more from 10 to 16. Table 1 illustrates the point.

Table 1. Stages of Equilibrium and Disequilibrium

| Even | Breakup | Calm | Withdrawal | Expansion | Transition | Equilibrium |
|------|---------|------|------------|-----------|------------|-------------|
| 1 | 2½ | 3 | 3½ | 4 | 4½ | 5 |
| 5 | 5½ | 6½ | 7 | 8 | 9 | 10 |
| 10 | 11 | 12 | 13 | 14 | 15 | 16 |

It suggest that in the ages between 2 and 16, each of three similar cycles starts with an age of equilibrium. This equilibrium is, thus, seen at 2, 5, and 10 years of age. In each cycle this initial phase of equilibrium is followed by a phase of disequilibrium in which behavior breaks down and becomes oppositional and uncomfortable. These phases of disequil-ibrium, customarily seen at 2½, 5½ and 11 are followed once again by easy stages, at 3, 6½ and 12 years, during which things tend to go well.

Once again, at a succeeding stage, behavior breaks down and is charac-terized by insecurity and withdrawal. The 3½ year old tends to be extremely insecure in every way. The 7 year old often seems unhappy, thinks that people do not like him. Thirteen withdraws and goes his own way.

Withdrawal is followed by expansion and, in general, behavior tends to be extremely expansive at 4, 8, and 14 years of age. Once again we come to stages of insecurity, disequilibrium, unpredictableness at 4½, 9, and 15 and then finally end up with equilibrium at 5, 10, and 16 years of age. Parents who are aware of and understand these stages are better equipped to deal with the ups and downs of childhood behavior and development.

### Norms of Behavior

Doctors at the Gesell Institute have established norms of motor, adaptive, language, and personal-social development by studying children over many years. However, the reader is urged to remember that *these norms are not set up as standards, they are a statistical device that gives an average which we can use to measure development.* In the book, *The Gesell Institute's Child from One to Six: Evaluating the Behavior of the Preschool Child,* Louise Bates Ames, Ph.D. states that "it is a gross misinterpretation of our normative work for any one to assume that we are saying that all children do or should develop in exactly the same way or at the same rate. Norms are merely guides to the way that behavior develops in general." Keeping the above statement in mind, here are the typical behaviors of a 4, 5, and 6 year old. These are intended to be very general:

## The Four Year Old

- is secure and comfortable
- has a love of adventure
- when angry, threatens to run away
- emotionally, laughs and cries too loudly
- boasts, brags, and exaggerates
- has discovered lies and profanity
- can stand on one foot for a few seconds

- can skip although can still not hop
- can catch a beanbag with hands only
- can learn to use roller skates
- can learn to ride a bicycle with training wheels
- can button large buttons and even lace his shoelaces
- can cut on a line with child scissors
- enjoys running, climbing, sliding, digging, and jumping
- can copy a square from a model at $4\frac{1}{2}$
- can count with correct pointing, 3 objects
- can print a few recognizable letters
- can copy the order of different colored or shaped stringed beads
- can match shapes such as squares, circles, and stars
- can build houses, stores, or forts with large blocks
- wants to lift heavy objects
- enjoys doll play with many roles
- loves to be silly
- has as many as 1,550 words in his vocabulary
- asks "why?" very often
- can give his correct age and number of siblings when asked
- can give first and last name and also names all of siblings by $4\frac{1}{2}$
- can repeat three digits correctly
- can correctly place a ball on, under, behind, in front of, and in back of, when asked
- answers correctly to the following questions: What must you do if you are hungry? sleepy? cold?
- for all his exuberance he basically appreciates boundaries and rules
- enjoys, is interested in, and admires other children
- toileting is an established routine
- can dress and undress without much help
- can put shoes on correct feet
- some can tie a knot but not a bow
- most can wash hands, face, and brush teeth

## The Transition from Four to Five

Four is, unquestionably, an age of exuberant expansion. Five is unquestionably a time of calm, temperate, pulled-in, close-to-home, behavior. But the child cannot and does not change from expansive and outgoing four to quiet and inwardized five overnight. The changes occur largely during the second half of the year that comes between the two stages. He is a bit more self-motivated than he was earlier. He is becoming aware of authority, and his awareness of "good" and "bad" things is strengthening. All in all, whatever is said about the child of this age, the opposite may be true since the 4½ year old is highly unpredictable. But if we keep in mind where the child has been and where he is going, it can help to define and understand where he is now.

## The Five Year Old

- quite conforming
- mother is the center of his world
- is comfortable within the prescribed bounds
- wants, means, and succeeds often at being good
- looks on the bright side of life
- has little interest in the new and strange
- very careful to attempt only what he can achieve
- a good judge of his own abilities
- he is not smug, but he *is* secure
- though not expansive in most things, he is expansive intellectually
- love to be read to, talked to, informed about things he does not know
- can skip, using his feet alternately
- can walk on tiptoe, five steps or more
- can stand on one foot, nine seconds or longer
- can achieve a broad jump as much as 27 inches
- more poised and less exuberant than at four
- loves tricycle or bicycle with small training wheels
- climbs with sureness
- enjoys stilts, roller skates, or jumping from heights
- hands as well as whole body become increasingly skilled
- likes to lace his shoes, button buttons, and "sew" wool through holes in a card
- appears more restrained and less active because he maintains one position for longer periods
- is a great "helper"
- can identify the hand he uses for writing
- can usually name his eyes, eyebrows, palm, elbow, thumb, and little finger

- in block building and other similar activities uses alternate hands but dominate hand is very present
- can stand on one foot for 12 seconds, throw a beanbag overhand, and can also catch a beanbag, hands against his chest.
- enjoys increasingly complicated jigsaw puzzles as well as sewing and carpentry.
- can copy a triangle
- can print his first name
- can count ten objects correctly and calculate within five; concept of numbers up through ten, is usually well established
- loves to cut, trace, draw, paste, string beads, and make things out of small pieces of paper or cloth.
- enjoys block play
- loves to talk
- his own questions are fewer than at four and more relevant
- likes new big words
- in Piaget's terms, is in the "preoperational" stage of thinking (this is explained and discussed in the next chapter)
- still has some difficulty distinguishing between fantasy and reality
- is beginning to try and figure things out for himself
- loves being read to more than ever
- his most enjoyed humor is in pretending that he is not going to do what his parents tell him to do
- makes up humorous, spontaneous stories
- loves praise and is pleased with his ability to imitate grown-up behavior
- plays *reasonably* well with siblings
- is a much easier playmate than he was at four, or than he will be at six
- food preferences are still rather marked, enjoys plain, simple cooking
- likes to take toy, animal, or doll with him to bed
- "reads," talks, or sings himself asleep
- frightening dreams are frequent
- can dress himself (except for tying shoelaces or difficult buttons), but usually doesn't

## The Transition from Five to Six

The beginnings of a definite change for the worse are evident around 5½ years of age. At 5, mother was the center of the child's world, but at 6, he is the center of his own world. He wants to be first, loved the most, and have the best of everything. "Brash," and "combative" are words that mothers often use to describe the child at this age. He also exhibits hesitancy and indecisiveness. Emotionally he may appear to be in a constant state of tension though, fortunately, is usually calmer at school than at home. Physically, too, there are signs of a breakup. The healthy five year old turns into a child with many colds, headaches, earaches, and stomachaches. He may even revert to toilet accidents when overexcited. Motor-wise he is more restless; his body seems less easier to control than it did at 5. All in all, organization is breaking up, and in a way, the child enjoys all of this upheaval. Unfortunately, any smooth stage of behavior, like the one seen at five, must break up before the child can reach a higher, more mature stage of stability. Thus the typical 6 year old resembles a 5½ year old at his worst. But that higher and more mature stage does come in most children around 6½ years of age, a great time of balance for many.

## The Six Year Old

- lives at opposite extremes, and whatever he does, he does the opposite just as readily
- is stubborn
- has considerable difficulty making up his mind, yet once made up it is hard to change it
- is the center of his world and wants things to go *his* way
- loves his mother but at the same time is trying to gain independence from her
- is demanding and difficult because he is still quite insecure and his emotional needs are very great
- if parents give patience and love to meet his needs, he can also be very giving
- can be enthusiastic and emotionally warm
- is constantly on the go, lugging, tugging, digging, dancing, climbing, pushing, and pulling
- awkwardness and misplaced energy often result in accidents

- has increased demand for fine motor tasks even though eye-hand behavior may now give him some difficulty
- loves to color, cut and paste, and paint
- likes to draw—people, houses, boats, trains, spaceships, and trees and flowers
- enjoys making things of paper, cardboard, or wood
- can print numbers from 1 to 11, half of the children this age can print from 1 to 20
- girls at 6, boys at 6½ can print both their first and last names
- letters and numbers are often reversed, and both tend to be large, labored, and uneven
- is more interested in the process (what he is doing at the moment) than in the final result
- can make a reasonably good copy of a diamond shape
- likes to talk and share his thoughts
- has good pronunciation and grammatical construction is fairly accurate
- can tell the day and the month of his birthday
- can repeat five digits in one of three tries
- can differentiate morning and afternoon
- can identify his left and right hand
- has a great curiosity, his questions seem endless
- is interested in the language of math and most can count to 30
- enjoys table games such as anagrams, dominoes, and simple card games that demand matching
- reading, whether being read to or spelling out letters for himself, is now an all-engrossing interest
- is learning to read not only single words but also combinations of words
- many now need a marker or to use their fingers when they read, otherwise they lose their place
- has a two-way nature; may be beautiful and bubbly one minute but difficult and quarrelsome the next
- he loves, depends on and needs his mother, yet when things go wrong he takes his frustration out on her
- he seeks and wants very much wants to be praised, but unfortunately, his behavior is often such that praise is hard to give
- at times seems to have a better relationship with his father, whom he

admires but somewhat fears, or with his teacher whom he tends to be much less involved than with his mother

- is a sore loser, and may even cheat or break up the game if he finds himself losing
- is extremely jealous and watches carefully to see that someone else does not get a bigger piece of cake or an extra turn
- is likely to deny his guilt if it will cause him to come out ahead
- tends to fidget and spill and reach across the table and chew with his mouth open. It is not unusual for him to fall out of his chair onto the floor.
- has great difficulty (girls especially) in deciding what to wear
- as he nears the age of 7, too-far-out 6 calms down, takes life easier and finds out that his interpersonal relationships are easier and more rewarding
- the age period of 6½ tends to emphasize most of the positive aspects of 6 with few of its difficulties. It is an age worth waiting for.

# Chapter 2

## COGNITIVE DEVELOPMENT

There are distinct stages of development in a child's thinking, and in each stage, there are characteristic ways of thinking. Swiss psychologist, Jean Piaget pioneered the area of study that deals with a child's intellect. He contends that the developmental stages are the same for all children and that each child will pass through the stages in the same order. The ages are only approximate and should not be considered fixed. Also, keep in mind that the passage from one stage to the next is not sudden or clear cut. A child may exhibit characteristics from two stages for several months before moving fully into the next stage of development.

The first stage of development is called the *sensorimotor stage.* This period occurs between birth to about two years. The child utilizes senses and motor reflexes to begin building knowledge of the world. He uses his eyes to see, his mouth to suck, and his hands to grasp. In this stage the child sees himself as the center of the world and believes all events are caused by him. If he can not see an object, it no longer exists. His frame of reference is the world of here and now.

By the end of the second year, the child begins to realize that just because an object can't be seen, it does not mean that the object is not there.

Sometime between the ages of two and a half and three, children make a leap in cognitive development that is as dramatic and clear cut as the emergence of a first tooth in physical development. In that short time span children learn that an object can be understood both as a thing itself and as a symbol of something else. This capacity to symbolize has long been recognized as a hallmark of human cognition. At this time the child begins to put words together with objects and begins to use symbols for things that are not present. It is at this point that the child is ready to enter the next stage of cognitive development.

The second stage is known as the *preoperational stage.* This is the stage a child is in when he enters school for the first time. It begins around age two and ends at approximately seven years of age. Language development begins to occur rapidly at this stage and there is much less dependence on the sensorimotor action characteristic with the first stage. A child in this stage makes judgments primarily on the basis of how things look. For instance, if you took two lumps of clay, exactly the same size, and molded one into a ball and one into a log, the preoperational child will tell you that the log is larger than the ball, even though he watched you make each object from equal sized lumps of clay. A preoperational child's knowledge is based only on what he is able to see. This is why it is so important for you to *model* a task or activity when teaching your child.

Piaget believed that until a child develops the *concept of reversibility*, the idea that the clay log can be molded back into a ball, he cannot understand the concepts of conservation. He must first be able to visualize the reversals.

Another well-known example of this stage of development is shown by giving a child two identical glasses containing the exact same amount of orange juice. When the orange juice from one of the glasses is poured into a shallow dish, the child sees the remaining glass as holding more orange juice than the dish. He cannot understand how the amounts can be the same when their appearances are so different. This concept is known as *conservation of quantity.*

The preoperational child thinks that everything has a reason or purpose and that every act of every person in his life, and in nature happens for a specific purpose. This accounts for the countless questions about how things work and why things happen. Also, a child in this stage of development believes that everyone thinks as they think and therefore act as they act for the same reasons. Because the preoperational child thinks the world revolves around him, he is unable to put himself in the place of others. He is unable to sympathize or empathize with others. This egocentricity also makes it difficult for him to grasp the concept of sharing.

The third stage of development is known as *concrete operations,* and takes place between the ages of about 7 to 12. Piaget, in his book *Genetic Epistemology* (New York: Columbia University Press, 1970), defines the term *operation* as follows: "First of all, an operation is an action that can be internalized; that is, it can be carried out in thought as well as executed materially. Second, it is a reversible action; that is, it can take place in one direction or in the opposite direction." So a concrete operational child begins to manipulate objects mentally rather than just depending on how things look. He understands that the orange juice and the clay have the same amounts because he reverses the process in his mind. A child in this stage is also capable of classifying objects, events, and time according to certain characteristics.

A concrete operational child is less egocentric and learns that other people have thoughts and feeling that may differ from their own. He is able to share with others and sympathize or empathize with his family and peers.

The last stage of development is known as the *formal operations* stage and represents the second part of operational intelligence. It begins around eleven years of age and extends to about fifteen years. During this stage, the child becomes capable of increasingly complex verbal problems and hypothetical problems and less dependent on the use of concrete objects to solve problems. He can think with symbols and has the ability to reason scientifically and logically. His experiences and development during this period lead him to adult reasoning.

There are no simple steps or sets of exercises which will move a child up the developmental ladder. It is a gradual, continual process occurring over a period of time and resulting from maturation and experiences. However, a stimulating environment can have positive results on a child's development.

American psychologist Jerome Bruner sees the enrichment of a child's environment as opening up enormous possibilities concerning his intellectual development.

Both Piaget and Bruner believed that the most valuable contribution a parent can make is to provide numerous and varied experiences and opportunities for discovery through the use of manipulative materials.

## LEFT BRAIN, RIGHT BRAIN

In recent years much research has been done on the brain and its two sides, which while they appear symmetrical, each has its own distinct function.

The left hemisphere is said to be in use for such skills as reading, writing, language, phonics, following directions, and listening. When you reach for a particular word to name an object, express a thought in speech, understand what your child is saying, you are calling on your left brain's unique language center. The left brain also seems to think logically and sequentially, breaking things down into steps. A left-brain child deduces things from a set of facts.

The right hemisphere is involved in math computation, spatial relationships, music, singing, creativity, art expression, and feelings and emotions. When you draw a picture or visualize where the new furniture will go in your living room, you are using your right brain's visual-spatial ability. It also processes subtle, nonverbal information such as tone of voice, body language, and facial expressions. You know when another person is annoyed because your right brain picks up cues (such as a shift in voice or body posture) and interprets them, but then sends the information to the left brain for verbalizing a response.

While left-brained people think in symbols, right-brained people deal with the concrete. They learn by doing, touching, moving, and being in the middle of things.

Although we all use both sides of our brain, we tend to use one side more than the other. It is in the dominant side that we process information first. If we learn to balance the strength of both sides of our brains, we come closer to realizing our full potential.

How do you determine if your child is right-brained? Simple observations will usually help. Many (but not all) right-brained children have trouble following directions. Also, they use a lot of gestures with their speech, have trouble with phonics, and like to take things apart and put them back together again. They like to doodle and draw, enjoy finding "hidden pictures," and arts and crafts activities. They are able to see pictures or shapes in clouds and "read" people's expressions and nonverbal cues. Right-brained children also enjoy moving objects (like checkers, silverware, blocks, etc.) around to form interesting patterns. Children more right-brain tend to prefer wholistic, visual activities, and may find it hard to describe their day in words. While right-handed children can be either left *or* right-brained, left-handed children are almost always right-brained.

A left-brain child is given to logical, language-oriented activity. They enjoy creating stories and scenarios during playtime, are able to explain events logically and sequentially, can solve problems by thinking aloud, and do things in a step-by-step manner. A left-brain child looks at and reads books for pleasure, likes wordplay, even jokes, and plays computer and video games and other games with a methodic approach (e.g., Mastermind, Battleship, Chinese checkers). Children more left-brain prefer activities with a language component or a beginning-to-end flavor. Working on jigsaw puzzles, they may try to fit pieces that clearly don't work.

Right or left-brain, there is no right or wrong. More often than not, your child will be some combination of both. Steven Sabat, Ph.D., a neuropsychologist at Georgetown University, believes that environment plays a huge role. "If you read to a child, the left brain must be active. If you're engaging the youngster in spatial activities, the right brain is involved." The big plus to finding your child's strengths is that you can identify weaknesses too. Helping a child to solve problems in ways that are not natural for him exercises the less-used hemisphere, narrowing the gap between the right and left brain. Here are some ways to strengthen your child's weaker half:

## Activities to Encourage Left Brain Skills

1. Cut out a picture from a magazine or a newspaper and take turns making up a story about it.
2. Play "What If." Ask your child to imagine what would happen if animals could talk, fish wore clothes or people didn't need to eat or sleep.
3. Do simple science experiments, encouraging your child to explain what's happening.
4. When "reading" picture books, ask your child to describe the action on the pages.
5. Encourage your child to collect rocks, shells, and leaves and other nature finds; then discuss how they can be sorted.
6. Ask your child how two objects are the same. And how are they different?

## Activities to Encourage Right Brain Skills

1. Help your child collect bits of paper, string, and shells to make a collage.
2. Ask your child to look for shapes in the clouds.
3. Encourage your child to create designs with geometric Colorforms or *The Tangram Magician* (Abrams), a book that comes with its own reusable vinyl stickers.
4. Ask your child to explain the emotions of people he sees in pictures, books, and magazines.
5. Read a story to your child and encourage him to draw a picture about it.

Sometimes problems will arise when a child who is very right-brained enters school and deals with a "left-brained curriculum," which is what most schools are. It would be most helpful to your child and you if you discovered this fact BEFORE he enters school.

If you suspect that your child is right-brained, you can adjust his activities to better suit his learning style. While your child is working on a skill, play soft music, it may help a right-brained child focus his attention longer and think better. Add movement into learning activities whenever possible. For example, sit on a set of stairs and move up to the next step with counting or learning the alphabet. Remember that right-brained children learn best by doing, touching, moving, and being in the middle of things. When he enters school, you may wish to inform his teacher of the ways that he learns best.

## HEREDITY VERSUS ENVIRONMENT

Two main forces—heredity and environment—account for the individual differences among children. Heredity is the process by which children inherit physical and mental traits from their parents. Environment consists of all the things in a child's surroundings that affect the child's development of the inherited traits.

Individual differences among children are caused by heredity and environment acting together, not separately. In general, heredity limits what the environment can do in influencing a child's development. For example, every child inherits a tendency to grow to a certain height. Not even the best environmental conditions will enable a child to grow much taller than this height. But children need the right conditions, including proper nourishment and exercise, to grow as tall as their heredity allows. Heredity and environment together thus determine the physical differences among children. The two forces together also account for individual differences in intelligence.

## DIFFERENCES IN INTELLIGENCE

How smart is your child? Does he have the curiosity and the brain power he'll need to do well in school and in the working world later on? There's probably not a parent alive who hasn't entertained those kinds of questions; after all, we all want our children to succeed, and a nimble mind has always been an important ticket to a fulfilling life.

As for how much parents can actually do about a child's intelligence, though, the answer is, not much, if the main goal is to jump-start his natural abilities so that he's talking at ten months or reading novels by age three. Although experts now see intellectual growth as a blend of nature and nurture, they also agree on something else: It can't be rushed. Just as most babies don't walk without first sitting upright and pulling themselves across the floor, the ability to learn unfolds gradually in a progression of steps that can't be skipped—steps that each child has to tackle at his own pace. In fact, parents who try to cut corners with crash courses and flash cards at age two often wind up jeopardizing other aspects of a child's development. Some possible problems: a precocious preschool reader who can't get along with peers or an overachieving third grader who winds up as a troubled, underachieving teen.

Consider the dramatic case of William James Sidis. His father was Professor Boris Sidis, one of the most brilliant psychologists of his time. He loved his little son very deeply, and had the longing that most fathers have of seeing him grow up to be a great man.

Most fathers just hope for such miracles, but Sidis thought he knew how to actually make it happen. As a psychologist, he had a theory that a child's brain was capable of far more learning than anyone suspected. So, while the child was still learning to balance himself on two feet, his father began teaching him how to read.

At the age of three, little Billy Sidis could read as well as most high school students. He wasn't permitted to read such simple books as *Treasure Island* or *Robin Hood.* Thanks to his father, this incredible three year old was reading books on algebra and thermodynamics.

When he was four, he wrote two 500-word essays, one in French and the other in English. A year later, his father was even more proud of his son when the five year old wrote a very learned treatise on anatomy. Sidis took the treatise to Harvard, where he himself lectured, and showed it to his colleagues. They were understandably amazed, but were even more amazed when the youngster showed them a method he had worked out for calculating the day of the week that any day in history would fall on.

At the age of eight, the boy had been taught by his father to read the classics in the original languages: Latin, Greek, French, Italian, and German. In between language lessons, he studied the violin and became an accomplished violinist.

By the time he was 10, he had written a textbook on geometry—in Greek. At 11, he was admitted to Harvard as an undergraduate student.

When he was 13, he was invited to lecture to the Harvard faculty on Einstein's theory of relativity.

The lecture at Harvard made him famous, and it made his father deeply proud. But it was at this time that Professor Sidis discovered something that he had never reckoned on. Out of his love for his son and his own great genius as a teacher, he had given him a mighty brain. But that gift was destroying him.

Suddenly Bill Sidis rebelled. He read no more books. Spoke no more foreign languages. Gave no more lectures. Instead, he took a routine job as an adding machine clerk and remained at that job for the rest of his life.

He lived only to the age of 46, dying in 1944 an old and weary man, serving as a sad example of the fact that the stages of learning must unfold gradually and that each child must be allowed to progress at their own pace.

## IQ TESTS

Differences in intelligence among children are usually measured by IQ (intelligence quotient) tests. These tests are designed to indicate a child's general mental ability in relation to other children of the same age. Each child's performance on the tests is rated by an IQ score. On most such tests, about two-thirds of all children score from 84 to 116 (average is considered 90–110). About a sixth score below 84, and a sixth score above 116.

The IQ scores of persons related by blood generally differ less than do the scores of unrelated persons. Some experts therefore conclude that general mental ability is largely inherited and is only slightly affected by environment. Other experts, however, believe that environment has a strong influence on a person's intelligence. Their view is supported by studies of *culturally deprived* children. Children are considered culturally deprived if their home life lacks the kinds of experiences that will help them profit from formal schooling. Many such children have an IQ score of below 80. It has been estimated that 15 or more points of IQ are experientially rather than genetically-based. The preschool experiences of these deprived children can cost them a significant portion of those points. But in a number of cases, culturally-deprived children greatly improved their score after receiving special training and encouragement in foster homes or in school.

It is probably fair to conclude that the IQ is not unmodifiable and that it is lowered by a variety of environmental impoverishments. On the other hand, there are clearly limits on the modifiability of intellectual development. There is no technique available by which the population of the usual home for mental defectives could be transformed into a group of average intelligence.

*Environmental enrichment* should be considered as something to accelerate the development of all children—as perhaps the television program *Sesame Street* has done. The practical implication of findings is that there is an efficient time for training skills if one is interested solely in obtaining the most effect from the least training. But it is dangerous to generalize much further.

One interesting finding in this area comes largely from work with animals. There is a critical period in the development of some behaviors in animals during which a particular kind of experience is necessary if the development is to proceed. Chicks normally learn to peck within a few days of hatching, and if a chick is kept in an incubator for only a few days he rapidly catches up when he is allowed free pecking opportunities. If, however, he is not given an opportunity to peck for two weeks after hatching, he will never learn the skill. Similarly, some behavior patterns seem to be learned in a very firm way through a small amount of experience at the critical period. Ducklings, for example, become inseparably attached to the object that they follow during the critical period soon after hatching. Normally this object is the mother duck, and thereafter the ducklings trail after the mother. But Konrad Lorenz showed that if the duckling is exposed to a person rather than the mother duck during the critical period, it will follow that person just as if it were the mother duck. This phenomenon is called imprinting and represents one extreme of a critical period.

The phenomenon of imprinting has never been clearly established in human children, but efforts to establish it have been far from exhaustive. Similarly, the hypothesis of critical periods in the child's life has been advanced frequently, but no clearly demonstrated example of a critical period has been produced. There seems no reason to suppose both phenomena cannot exist in human development.

Some experts question the usefulness of IQ tests on the grounds that they do not measure basic mental skills. These experts point out that intelligence involves a variety of separate powers, such as memory, logic, evaluation, and originality. A child may have little ability in some of these areas but exceptional talent in one or more other areas. The critics therefore believe that children should be tested and evaluated for each mental skill separately. Likewise, American psychologist Howard Gardner suggests that instead of thinking of a person's intellectual level in terms of some one specific number, intelligence should be considered as taking many different forms: linguistic, logical-mathematical, spatial, musical, bodily kinesthetic, interpersonal, and intrapersonal. Many psychologists now accept this approach.

# SECTION II
# AT HOME

*The strength of a nation derives from the integrity of the home.*
Confucius

# Chapter 3

## YOUR CHILD'S FIRST TEACHER IS YOU

Years ago, you were ready for kindergarten if you knew how to put on a jacket and share your toys. But these days, readiness for kindergarten is much more complicated, and parents are the first and most important teachers of their children. Readiness is the parent's responsibility. Your attitude towards this fact has an enormous impact on your child whether you are aware of it or not. The correlation between a child's success in school and the degree of parental support that a child receives is indisputable.

But what does it mean to be a supportive parent? It is actually quite simple. Parents must instill in their child a love and respect for learning, for themselves, and for others. To do this, parents don't necessarily have to be well educated themselves. Teaching a child to love and respect does not require a degree. And self-worth can certainly take a child farther than "natural intelligence." It is a self-fulfilling prophecy: The child who is told and believes that he can succeed, will succeed. And likewise, the child who is told he is stupid, dumb, or slow will perform below his potential.

Here are some simple but effective ways in which you can prepare your child for a successful school experience. These ideas are discussed in more detail with specific suggestions in the chapters that follow.

- Maintain a specific schedule at home. There should be designated times for meals, bedtime, play and chores. This teaches a child order and self-discipline. Children need and expect limits. When there are none, the child cannot trust his environment or experience his full potential for emotional growth and development. A child does best with consistency and established routines.
- Read to your child EVERYDAY. Don't claim that you don't have the time. Make the time. Reading to your child is the single most important thing you can do to ensure that she will learn to read.

Five minutes a day is all it takes. Even the back of a cereal box or a street sign on the drive home will do.

- Take your child to the museum, the library, and historical areas. This makes learning fun and peeks your child's natural curiosity. It will instill a love of learning for its own sake.

- Talk to your child, not just AT her. Try to answer your child's questions in a way that will be meaningful to her. If you dodge her questions or give vague uninterested cues to her, she will pick up on this and soon her natural curiosity will be squelched, sometimes forever. During conversations, ask your child thought-provoking questions.

- Build on your child's interests. Family outings or a special day with Mom and Dad can be built on that interest. With a little research and encouragement on your part, one simple interest can blossom into many areas and become a source of knowledge, competence, and responsibility in which your child can shine.

- Give your child plenty of praise and encouragement. Find at least one thing to praise your child for EVERYDAY.

- Provide a sense of family history and communicate values. Besides passing on family history, family stories also teach values—what you and other family members consider important, such as hard work, a sense of humor, good manners, or patriotism. It is primarily from us that our children learn social skills, attitudes toward work and play, and definitions of success, all of which play a big part in their growth.

- Monitor your children's TV watching. TV can be a wonderful learning aid, however hours of unsupervised TV or Nintendo is like putting your child's brain on hold. Select one or two appropriate shows together. Then, whenever possible watch the show together and discuss it afterwards. Ask specific questions such as "What color was the car that Ernie drove?"

## DISCIPLINE

The discipline of children has been the subject of countless books and certainly the subject of discipline could cover much more than the few pages devoted to it in this chapter. This information is meant to be a very basic capsule of the disciplining of children in general. If you are experiencing problems disciplining your children, you should seek additional information from a reliable and competent source experienced in childhood education and or psychology. There are many excellent books written by experienced educators. Please do not rely solely on the advice of friends, relatives and the like, as the consequences of this may not present the desirable outcome.

Many parents fail to realize the important fact that *there is a critical period during the first four or five years of a child's life when she can be taught proper attitudes. These early concepts become rather permanent. When the opportunity of those years is missed, however, the prime receptivity usually vanishes, never to return.* A parent cannot simply hope for these attitudes and behavior, *they must be taught.* Heredity does not equip a child with proper attitudes; children will learn what they are taught. Respectful and responsible children result from families where there is the proper combination of discipline *and* love.

One of the most well respected authorities on discipline is Dr. James Dobson, author of the book *Dare To Discipline.* This book has been used in schools across America as the guide for handling discipline. In this book, Dr. Dobson states the following:

> I am thoroughly convinced that the proper control of children can be found in a reasonable, common sense of philosophy, where five key elements are paramount.
>
> 1. Developing respect for the parents is the crucial factor in child management. It is most important that a child respect his parents, not for the purpose of satisfying their egos, but because the child's relationship with his parents provides the basis for his attitude with all other people.
>
> 2. The best opportunity to communicate often occurs after punishment. After the emotional ventilation, the child will often want to crumple to the breast of his parent, and he should be welcomed with open, warm loving arms. At that moment you can talk heart to heart. You can tell him how much you love him and how important he is to you. You can explain why he was punished and how he can avoid the difficulty next time. Parental warmth after punishment is essential to demonstrate to the child that it was his behavior, and not the child himself, that the parent rejected.
>
> 3. Control without nagging. Yelling and nagging at children can become a habit, and an ineffectual one at that! Have you ever screamed at your child, "This is the last time I'm going to tell you, 'this is the last time' "? Parents often use anger to get action, instead of using action to get action.
>
> 4. Don't saturate the child with excessive materialism. Pleasure occurs when an intense need is satisfied. If there is no need there is no pleasure. A glass of

water is worth more than gold to a man dying of thirst. The analogy to children should be obvious. If you never allow a child to want something, he never enjoys the pleasure of receiving it.

    5. Avoid extremes in control and love. The "middle ground" of love and control must be sought if we are to produce healthy, responsible children.

Perhaps one of the most common mistakes parents make concerning discipline is by *being inconsistent.* One day it is acceptable for the child to throw a tantrum and scream and cry and the next day it is not. The parent yells, "if you do that one more time I'm going to spank you!", the child commits the offensive act again, and is *not* spanked but instead yelled at repeatedly. Thus she learns that her parent will not really do what she says she will, so she learns that she can do as she pleases and the consequences will be yelling and screaming or idle threats, which she has already become accustomed to, and ignores anyway.

The answer lies in this simple technique: identify the rules well in advance; let there be no doubt about what is and is not acceptable. And second, let the child know what the consequences will be if she chooses to break the rules and then *stick to your word and carry out the consequence no matter what!* An example of this technique would be, "Marianne, if you don't pick up your toys before supper, you can't watch TV after supper." Thus if Marianne quickly ran around the room to pick her toys up *after* supper, her mother should not give in to her but rather stand firm and not allow her to watch TV. If a parent is firm and consistent constantly, the child learns to trust and respect what the parent says and has a predictable and secure environment in which she can grow and develop normally.

Punishment is not something you do *to* the child, but rather something you do *for* the child. Your attitude to your child should be, *"I love you too much to let you misbehave this way!"*

Discipline involves setting limits, teaching by example, and sticking to your rules. When you do need to punish your child, use the "time out" technique. Have her spend a specified period of time sitting in a chair or corner of the room. Never make a child sit in a place that's scary or dangerous. During the "time out" period, the child is not allowed to talk or play.

"Time out" can be started when a child is about 18 months old, and it is most successful for children who are at least two. One minute per year of age is a good rule of thumb, so a two year old's time out lasts two minutes from the time she starts sitting in the chair. This works better than spanking because you can use it consistently.

Children will act out until they are understood. The most successful parents are those who have the skill to get behind the eyes of the child, seeing what she sees, thinking what she thinks, feeling what she feels. Unless parents can master this ability, children will continually react in a harmful manner.

## TEACHING YOUR CHILD
## THE BASICS OF SELF-CONTROL

The child without self-control finds life simply miserable. If her behavior is uncontrollable, parents and teachers must dislike her because they are always angry and correcting her, her peers avoid her, and she even dislikes herself. She will probably fail to get into college and will barely finish high school. Without self-discipline, her chances for a career are even worse. Many parents assume that self-control will automatically improve with age, yet for most children, this is not true. By nature, kids are spontaneous and impulsive. They are feeling creatures who act first and think later, which makes them both delightful and difficult.

Self-control and self-discipline are necessary elements of the foundation for learning. Without them, a child can never reach her full potential.

Here are seven steps that parents can take to help their children develop the self-control and maturity that will make their delightful moments far outnumber the difficult ones.

### Step 1: Accepting Responsibility by Doing Chores

One of the ways children can gain maturity best is by having responsibilities to fulfill. You can begin to convey a sense of responsibility by assigning meaningful duties that will make your child feel like a contributing member of the family. Simple duties include setting the table, clearing the table, sorting the laundry (whites from darks), making the bed, putting toys back where they belong after playtime, and helping unload and put away the groceries. If you have pets in the house, assign your child to monitoring or even filling the water bowl. If you have a yard, assign your child a simple chore outside, such as picking up small branches.

The difficult part of this step is not in the assigning of chores, but in making sure that they are carried out. If they are not, parents need to be consistent with discipline and the child should know clearly what the results will be if they fail to complete the task. This instills the importance of completion as a value and helps children develop the perseverence necessary to follow through. Many parents scold and yell, but there are never any imposed consequences. The punishment need not be severe, but it should be discussed beforehand and administered consistently. For instance, if your child fails to make her bed one morning, you might assign her the task of making your bed as well as hers the next day. (This requires parental patience.) Don't "fix" it if children forget their chores. Yes, it is much easier to make the bed yourself while mumbling a few gruff words, but this does the child no good and does nothing towards teaching responsibility except for the incorrect notion that "it's OK if I don't do it, someone else will do it for me."

One of the hardest lessons a child can learn is that life is not fair and we all have to do things we don't want or like to do. *Talk* this idea out with your child in a caring concerned way, when the opportunity presents itself. Also, use your own life as an example of these concepts. ("Mom doesn't always feel like cooking dinner and cleaning up afterwards, but it is my job and I have to do it, even when I don't feel like it.") Children who don't learn these basic lessons have the hardest time as adults.

In spite of what they say and how they behave, children don't really like getting away with neglecting their responsibilities; it leaves an unpleasant feeling inside when you let yourself—and others—down.

Also, don't overdo praise. It is generally not a good idea to heap piles of praise on a preschooler for doing her duty. The expectation that everyone does his or her share should be communicated matter-of-factly, with gentle but low-key appreciation. When high praise, applause, or rewards are given, a child is likely to continue to do the tasks—but only if rewards are forthcoming.

Parents' patience and support in helping them meet their obligations will serve children for the rest of their lives.

### Step 2: Sticking to a Schedule

Sometimes children with the best intentions fail to carry out their responsibilities simply because they lose track of time. Parents can foster maturity in children by planning and sticking to a specific schedule with time for important obligations set aside. This takes discipline on your part also, but if you can make yourself and your child stick to it for six weeks, it soon becomes habit and a source of pride. Children need and expect limits, they perform much better when they know WHAT is expected of them and WHEN. Try to set a specific time for:

- chores
- homework
- meals
- and most importantly, bedtime.

One reminder—a schedule includes limits on television viewing as well.

## Step 3: Listening to Directions

Every school teacher has been faced with the frustrations of children who simply don't listen. Listening is a skill that must be taught and learned. A child who has not mastered this skill will have trouble performing well in school. Here are some techniques to help develop listening skills.

1. Ask your child to carry out silly commands that require careful listening such as, "Put your hands on your head, then turn around and clap three times." Make a game out of it and award points for each successfully completed command.

2. Take your child outside to a place where nature sounds can be heard. Ask her to close her eyes and be perfectly quiet for two minutes and listen to all the sounds there are to be heard. Afterwards, discuss what was heard. You can also play this game in traffic with the car windows down or waiting in line at the store. We are much more aware of sounds without our vision.

3. Ask your child to repeat your instructions after you give them. This is a trick used by many teachers.

4. Read a simple short story to your child and then ask her to tell it back to you. Cue her by saying, "And then what happened?"

5. Listen to and memorize songs and sing them together in the car, while you're cooking, etc.

6. Read a series of numbers for your child and ask her to repeat them back to you. Start with two-number sequences and increase as your child is ready.

7. Teach your child a simple poem by saying one verse at a time and having her repeat it back to you.

8. Say a word and ask your child to say a word that rhymes with it.

9. Say two words that are either exactly the same or slightly different and have your child tell you if they are the same or different. (Example: ball and bad; sit and sat)

10. Say three words, two of which begin with the same sound, and ask your child to tell you which begins with a different sound? (Example: ball, moon, bed)

11. Play the old popular game "I'm going on a trip." Begin by saying, "I'm going on a trip and I'm taking my car." The next person has to add one item to the list, so they would say, "I'm going on a trip and I'm taking my car and my sun glasses." Continue repeating the first two items and add a new one each turn.

12. Play Simple Simon.

## Step 4: Abiding by the Rules

At school, children are taught a set of rules and expected to abide by them. Often when a child has trouble with this concept, it is because there are no structured rules at home.

Two simple examples of this involve putting away toys and keeping track of belongings. At school, when a child takes off her jacket, she is expected to hang it in the appropriate place. When she is through with an activity or toy, she is expected to clean up and replace the items to their proper place. Parents should expect this behavior at home also. Even a three year old can put her shoes in the closet and put her toys back in the toy trunk. This responsibility should be carried out *daily*. Soon it will be habit and will instill a sense of order as well as respect for rules.

## Step 5: Taming Angry Feelings

Many parents reinforce bad behavior by giving their children attention only when they misbehave. Look for times when your child behaves well and then lavish her with praise. Soon, she will get the message that "mom gives me attention when I am good," and she will behave accordingly. Teachers often seek out the good behavior in their classroom and ignore the child who is misbehaving. When the misbehaving child notices that the well behaved child is being praised, she quickly strives to copy that behavior, thus receiving the praise she was searching for in the first place. This is satisfying to her, so she no longer feels the need to misbehave.

If your child has a temper problem, remember that she will respond better when taught to do something rather than not to do it. For example, instead of throwing a fit when she can't have her way, teach her to take a deep breath and count to 10 before she speaks. (This works well for parents too.) Or teach her to simply say (not yell), "It makes me angry when you do that." The trick is not to suppress our feelings but to deal with them rationally and appropriately. Parents need to remember to set a good example and not lose it themselves when a child loses control. Remain calm and firm.

In all cases, remember to make sure your child gains attention by behaving, not by misbehaving.

## Step 6: Patience Takes Practice

Children often lose control when they feel frustrated by their own limitations. Parents can help by teaching tactics to use in these stressful situations. Stay with a child while she tackles a task that requires patience, such as putting together a difficult puzzle or untangle a knot in a shoestring. As she works on the problem, describe the things she does that demonstrate self-control and problem solving techniques. When she realizes these differences in her behavior she will make better choices. Use lots of compliments like, "Way to go!, That's the way to stick to it!" or "Good, the first way didn't work, so now you are trying another way." Just as you use praise to reinforce good behavior, use it to reinforce patience and perseverence.

If she becomes really frustrated with an activity, teach her how to cope with it. Suggest that she clasp her hands together and squeeze as hard as she can, then exhale and release the squeeze. Have her take a deep breath and say to herself, "OK, it's time to calm down." Then you can praise her, and start over again. If after 10 or 15 minutes, she is still frustrated and getting nowhere, take a break from the activity and try again later.

## Step 7: Delaying Gratification

This is without a doubt the toughest lesson to learn. Even parents have a hard time with this one. What child wouldn't rather watch TV before she does her chores?

When teaching children to think ahead, talk about the immediate benefits of making good choices. Telling a child to do her homework so she can go to college when she grows up is meaningless to her. Talk about the here and now and why she will be glad if she does her homework now. Don't allow your child to "beg" her way out of it. Stand firm and calm and then proceed as if there is no question that right this minute we are going to do homework. Afterwards, praise your child and encourage her to realize how glad she is that the task is completed.

Don't forget the impact *your* actions have on your child. Remember the wise old sayings, "Actions speak louder than words" and "Attitudes are caught, not taught."

Of course, all of this is easier said than done. We are all human and that means we aren't always disciplined. Though we want our children to become mature, we can't expect more of them than we do of ourselves. The point is that we have a goal in mind which we are working towards. Teaching your child self-discipline is laying a firm foundation from which she can achieve any goal she chooses in life.

# Chapter 4

# TEN CONCEPTS TO TEACH
# YOUR CHILD AT HOME

There has been an incredible amount of material written on the evils of "forced learning." I in no way condone that practice. The activities in this chapter are presented in hopes that they will get your child to expand his or her present capabilities in a way that is fun and nonthreatening. To learn and grow in a way that is so subtle that the child does not realize that he is actually "learning." The most important thing you should remember when working with your child is this: *If it's not fun, stop immediately!* Don't force your child to learn a skill or task that he is not ready or willing to try. This will destroy the fun of learning for him, and possibly change his attitude about learning in school also.

## TEN CONCEPTS TO TEACH YOUR CHILD AT HOME

There are several concepts that are important for the preschool-age child. These concepts are the basis for the majority of the kindergarten curriculum. By exposing your child to these concepts, you are helping him to become a good and confident learner and easing his transition from home to school. If he is a confident learner, he will be eager to try new activities and experiences.

These concepts can be taught in and around the house, in everyday situations, and require no special materials. When your child learns through using his natural environment, and by doing and playing, the learning has more meaning for him than the child who is taught through flash cards and memorization. Remember that a young child has to move from concrete to abstract. If he is simply memorizing how to count it has no meaning for him. But if he can be an active participant in a counting activity, he begins to understand the correspondence between numbers and counting.

Before you begin teaching any of the concepts, consider these tips for getting the most out of any learning task or activity:

### Keep Learning Time Pleasant

Use smiles, hugs, and praise to keep a child working. Change your voice tones. Use an excited voice. Keep the task interesting.

### Their Own Environment

Use your own home, your own neighborhood to help your child learn. As much as possible, turn daily chores and activities into opportunities for teaching. As you cook, repair, shop, clean, visit, prepare, etc., find the learning games that can be played naturally in each situation. By simply explaining to your child what it is that you are doing at any given moment, you are expanding his horizons and teaching him something new. "I am mixing the eggs with the flour to make the pancakes."

### Be a Word Giver

Always use words to help your child learn language that describes what is happening. Children need you to teach them the names of people, objects, actions, and feeling. Be a word giver. Give words about experiences. Learning is easier when we have words to describe what we are doing, seeing or feeling.

### Children Learn by Doing and Playing

Children learn well when they can move around and touch. Acting-out ideas aids learning. For young children, play is the natural way to learn. During play, things happen, and as things happen, children learn. Colors blend, clay dries, a wagon tips over. Children discover that things change. This leads to *What-if-I-change-this?* games. Many children take the next step, *What-if-I-do-this-next?* games. In this way they find out what will happen if they change the way they are using something.

### Let Your Child Be the Teacher

Occasionally, when you are looking at a book about some subject your child is interested in, let your child be the teacher, and say, "Oh, tell me about this picture." "What is that?" Trade roles and let your child teach you for a change. Your child will love the feelings of self-esteem and credibility that this situation creates.

**Don't Compare Your Child with Others**

*Don't worry about what someone else's child did at this age!* Plan learning games for *your* child. Children are all special. They do not learn things in exactly the same way or at the same time as other children.

**And Most Importantly . . .**

Above all, *enjoy being your child's teacher.* Catch your child doing well at learning. Use lots of praise to let your child know you are proud and pleased. Your encouragement is like vitamins that nourish your child's self-esteem. Your enjoyment in working together at learning games will build healthy emotions as well as healthy positive attitudes toward learning.

# 1. GROUPING

Young children find it difficult to understand why things go together. You should help your child understand that some things go together because they look, feel, sound, or taste the same. For instance, a knife, fork, and spoon go together because they are *used together.* A boat, ship, and canoe go together because they are *used for the same reason.* An apple, firetruck, and valentine could be grouped together because they are all the *same color.*

You can turn this into a game like the TV show *Sesame Street* has done. Four objects are shown, three of which belong together. The child has to pick out the object that does not belong and tell why it doesn't belong. You could play this game with props, pictures, or verbally. Here are a few examples:

- A firetruck, police car, ambulance, and sports car.
- An apple, banana, orange, and egg.
- A shirt, pants, socks and blanket.
- A crayon, pen, pencil and flashlight.

When choosing your groups include characteristics such as the way they feel, the shape, and the size in addition to the ones listed above. The older your child, the more subtle the differences should be.

A variation of this game would be to pick a subject and ask your child to name as many objects that go with that group as possible. Some examples of groups include sports, clothing, animals, food, furniture and appliances, and family members.

In order to make groups, children need to sharpen their noticing skills. You can help your child *compare* the way things look, taste, or sound. You can point out how they are the same or different. You might start by saying something like, "How are a cat and a dog the same?" Then help your child reason that they are both animals with four legs and a tail. They both make good pets, and give birth to babies, etc. Next ask, "How are a dog and a cat different?" (They make different noises, dogs are usually bigger, and cats have sharp claws and soft fur, etc.) By doing this, children begin to *notice more details.* They are then ready to notice the subtle difference between letters. This is a necessary skill in beginning reading.

You can use anytime or place for this game. Simply choose two objects and discuss their similarities and differences. Start out with very obvious differences, and after a time you can gradually help your child to notice more subtle differences.

Help your child to understand that there are smaller groups inside of the big groups. For example: The animal group includes dogs (dalmations, beagles, etc.); cats (siamese, persian); bears (polar, koala, panda) and so on. The food groups include fruits, vegetables, meats, grains, diary. The clothing group could include summer, winter, outdoor, indoor, job-related (fireman, policeman).

By helping your child to understand these separate parts in a big group you are giving him a necessary skill for beginning reading. When he begins to read he will learn that letters are parts of words, which are parts of sentences, which make up stories.

Mathematics begins with an understanding of categories; of what goes with what. Loading the dishwasher, sorting and folding laundry, and putting toys away can all be turned into sorting or grouping games.

The following grouping activities are useful in developing *visual discrimination,* a skill needed for beginning reading:

- Using six pennies, line them up in the pattern: heads, tails, tails, tails, tails, heads. Point to the first penny and ask your child to find another one that looks just like it. Change the order; try using four heads and two tails, or use nickels, dimes, or quarters for variation.
- As you are driving or walking, point out a familiar traffic sign (STOP, YIELD, and so on). Encourage your child to look for more of them. EXIT signs on the interstate give lots of opportunities to play this game. Have your child count how many he sees.
- Cut out, in pairs, swatches of wallpaper or fabric, and glue them

onto index cards or pieces of cardboard for easy handling. Mix and have your child pair up the swatches. Later on you can use them for a memory game of concentration.

## 2. SEQUENCE

Help your child learn logical order using blocks, buttons, beads, cubes, empty boxes or cans, pots and pans, scrapes of material and anything else you can find around the house. Also, there are many puzzles on the market that help in teaching this skill. Some simple ideas include:

- Collect a set of five buttons or circles of paper of varying sizes. Ask your child to find the smallest one. Then arrange the rest in order from smallest to largest, left to right. Discuss what you have done, mix the buttons up and ask your child to find the largest button. See if he can arrange the rest in order from largest to smallest, left to right.
- Make a pattern using toothpicks or dry cereal pieces, and have your child duplicate it.
- String different colored beads or cereal into a pattern and have your child duplicate the pattern exactly. Start with 3 or 4 beads per pattern, and add more when he is ready.
- Cut paper towel tubes into different sizes. Have your child arrange the pieces into a row from the shortest to the tallest.

## 3. UNDERSTANDING TIME

Young children get very confused by time references such as yesterday and tomorrow. Help your child become aware of time words. Time words include *first, next, last, after,* and *before.* Ask your child questions to find out how well he understands time words. Sometimes ask a silly question. (Do this when you are fairly sure the child knows the correct answer.)

Here are some sample questions:

Which do we take off *first,* our shoes or our socks?
I put on my coat. What do you think I'll do *next?*
When you get dressed in the morning, what do you put on *last?*
What do I do *after* I put toothpaste on my toothbrush?
What should we do *before* we eat dinner?

Help your child think about each step in an activity. Help him see how the steps take place in a certain orderly way. For example, when we wash our hair, *first* we wet our hair. *Then* we put some shampoo in our hand. *Next* we soap and scrub our hair and head, and *last* we rinse and dry our hair.

A simple way to teach this would be to cut out your child's favorite cartoon from the Sunday paper. Cut the cartoon strip into 3 pieces and let your child put them in order: first, next, and last.

When your child begins school, he will be expected to put a story in order using the words, *first, next,* and *last.* You are helping him prepare for this skill when you use these words in everyday situations.

## 4. POSITIONAL WORDS

Many parents think that children naturally understand the meaning of *top* or *bottom, outside* or *around.* But your child needs to *act* out these positions to truly understand their meaning. Using games you can tell your children to get *under* the table or *behind* the door. In this way they begin to understand what space and place ideas mean.

Children enjoy playing this learning game with a favorite doll or stuffed animal. Explain to your child that you will play a pretend game with his doll. "Bert wants to sit *on* the chair. Now Bert wants to get *down*. Now Bert wants to hide *behind* the chair. And now he is tired and wants to sit *next* to the chair. Can you sit *beside* Bert? Now Bert wants to hide again *under* the chair." And so on.

Using a box large enough for your child to climb into, you can teach these words: *into, outside, around, under, over, upside-down, on,* and *beside.* Other positional words to teach your child include *top, bottom,* and *corner.*

## 5. BEGINNING MATH CONCEPTS

Most of us tend to concentrate our preschool "curriculum" at home on learning to read. We don't usually provide an equally rich opportunity for our children to absorb numbers. It is important that we make an extra effort to offer lots of manipulative experiences. *Handling objects is extremely important for the development of a child's ability to think and learn in logical patterns.* In fact, in preschools and elementary schools, using manipulatives is the dominant approach to understanding math facts and concepts such as addition, subtraction, multiplication, and division.

Preschool children are always so proud of themselves when they learn to count to 10 or sing a number song. That's OK. It is a chance for them to show off and feel good about themselves. But more than the ability to recite, what we want our children to have is a concept of what numbers are. For example, if a child can't tell that there are three glasses of juice on the table or four people in the car, then knowing how to count obviously doesn't mean anything to him.

What you need to do is to expose him to numbers and number concepts early, giving the numbers meaning. When you hand your child two crackers, say, "Here are two crackers. One," as he takes the first one, and "two," as he takes the second. The more you use numbers, the sooner he will grasp the concept that each number corresponds to a certain amount.

Encourage your child to *touch* each object while counting. Count pennies, or buttons. Count steps in walking. Count the number of people in the room. Count the number of clothes you toss in the washing machine or the number of bites of cereal he eats.

Help your child use a calendar to count off the days in a month before his birthday or some other special event.

Use words like *first, second,* and *third.* As you dry dishes or put away groceries, count with your child.

As you set the table or do housework, try simple addition with your child. "One spoon, plus two more spoons makes three spoons." "We had four apples and you ate one, so now there are three apples left."

Play card games such as "Go Fish" which use counting and numbers.

On blank index cards, write the numbers from 0–10 in words as well as the numerals. Give your child a pile of paper clips and ask him to attach the corresponding number of clips to each card.

Cut out cardboard "feet" (trace your child's) and number them from 0 to 10. Arrange them in order and let your child walk on them, counting aloud as he goes.

Make a large number line (0–10) using chalk on the driveway (it will wash away), and have your child stand on any number he chooses. Ask him to move ahead 4 spaces and tell you where he is. Simply state the fact involved ("3" plus "4" equals "7").

Some basic math vocabulary you may want to expose your child to:

- all vs. none
- more vs. less
- empty vs. full
- dozen
- many
- few
- fewer
- more
- single
- double
- triple
- several

## 6. LEARNING THE DIFFERENCE
## BETWEEN REAL AND SEEMING CHANGE

Children are often fooled by the way things look. You may lay a string out straight or curvy. Either way, the string is just as long. The curled up string *looks* shorter. But it is just as long as the string when it is straight. This was discussed in Chapter 2, as *conservation of quantity*. When the child is given two identical glasses containing the same amount of orange juice, he cannot understand how the amounts can be the same when the juice from one of the glasses is poured into a shallow dish. He sees the remaining glass as holding more orange juice than the dish. You can help your child figure this out. Your child will learn when changes fool him into thinking the length or amount is different, and he can learn to notice them carefully.

The bathtub is a great place for experimenting with water and pouring and discovering how the *conservation of quantity* works (also working with play-dough and clay).

By cooking with your child, he sees that an egg looks very different depending on how it is cooked. It actually changes. And that dough turns into cookies and batter into cake. Food tastes different before and after cooking. Freezing, boiling, mashing, melting, frying, and baking all change the way food looks.

Also when cooking, your child learns about measurement and sequence, two very important concepts for a preschooler.

## 7. LEARNING TO USE BODY PARTS TOGETHER

Young children need to learn to use arm and leg and eye muscles together skillfully. They need to coordinate these muscles in games such as tricycle riding, skipping, jumping, or when they hit, roll, kick, or throw a ball. Using these muscles together successfully makes them feel good about themselves and their bodies.

When children learn to use fingers and hands and eyes together smoothly they have a good chance to—

- eat with forks and spoons without much mess
- drink without spilling
- clean up and put toys and play materials away neatly
- dress themselves using buttons and zippers correctly
- learn how to print letters and numerals
- play games such as: stringing beads, or threading a shoe lace through punched holes in a cardboard picture, or building block towers.
- prepare simple snacks, such as spreading peanut butter on a cracker
- start collections and arrange them (such as rocks, bugs, stamps, or postcards)
- use blunt scissors to cut out interesting pictures to collect or paste in a homemade book.

Make sure that your child is given numerous activities to develop to his maximum physical potential.

## 8. LEARNING TO REASON

To succeed in school, a child needs to know how to think and give reasons. Your child needs your help in learning *how* to think and *how* to find reasons in order to solve problems. The activities listed can give you a chance to help your child think in a more organized way.

Help your child use the *if-then* and *because* in thinking about what to do and why. "My *Big Wheels*® can't fit through the door *because* it is too fat and wide. But *if* I turn my *Big Wheels* on its side, *then* it will be skinny enough to fit through the door."

Help your child learn to answer questions clearly and correctly. Help your child learn to ask questions that make sense and help him to learn to think hard about experiences. Ask questions that start with the five question words. Here are some examples:

*What*   What street do we live on?
       What do we cook soup in?
       What color is grass?
       What does a mommy do? What does a daddy do?
*Where*  Where would we go to find a bus?
       Where would you go to see an elephant?
       Where are some swings?
       Where can you buy a hamburger?
*When*   When do we eat breakfast?
       When do we get our clothes on and get dressed?
       When do you see the streets all wet?
       When do you need to help set the table?
*How*    How does a puppy dog show you that he is happy?
       How can you reach a small toy that rolled under the couch?
       How do we make toast?
       How do you make a sand pie?
       How can you keep your feet dry if it's wet outside?
       How can you paint without getting your clothes messy?
       How does a cat drink milk?

How questions help a child think in an orderly way. For example, How do we make a bed? *First* we smooth the sheets. *Then* we put on the blanket. *Next* we put the bedspread on top and *last* we smooth it all around.

*Why*    Why do we drink water?
       Why do we need a sink?
       Why do we have feet?
       Why do you need two children to make the see-saw work?
       Why do babies cry?
       Why does your shirt need buttons?
       Why do we look both ways before we cross the street?

Ask questions similar to these that will help him figure out why an event has occurred and what he can do about it:

- If you were helping me with the dishes and you noticed your sleeve was soaking wet, what do you think would have happened?
- If we found a tiny baby bird on the ground and it could not fly, what do you think must have happened?
- If you are building with your blocks and try to put a very large block on top of a small one, what do you think might happen?
- If you don't put your shoes where they belong after you take them off, what might happen?

## 9. USING IMAGINATION

Albert Einstein once said, "Imagination is more important than knowledge." How true that statement is, especially when applied to a preschooler. A child's mind once stretched by a new idea, never regains its original dimension.

A rich imagination helps us become more creative and interesting. Artists, musicians, and actors all use their imaginations. You can help your child think more creatively and develop his imagination.

Children love to play pretend games. Encourage your child to do this and even join in with him. Provide him with plenty of "props." A blanket thrown over two chairs becomes a "fort." Old clothes helps him pretend to be different people. A large appliance box becomes a "house." Empty cereal boxes and cans are transformed into "the grocery store."

Try "cloud watching" with your child on a warm day. Take turns imagining what each cloud shape could be. Take turns imagining how toys and objects could be used differently. For example, a paper bag could be a hat, a box with a top could be a lunch box, and so on.

Take turns making up stories and telling them to each other. Your child will do this better if you tell a story first. Try to include things that are special to the child, such as his blanket, or a pet, or even his name. Add a certain amount of silliness, which your child will love. When it's your child's turn to tell his story, write it down for him and read it back to him. This makes written language more meaningful for him.

## 10. LANGUAGE AND READING

You are the most important person in giving the gift and power of language to your child. *Talk* about things that happen. Help your child to learn to use words to describe what has happened or what *will* happen. Have your child describe what went on in play or what the child is wishing or feeling.

Keep language a loving family activity. A child that hears harsh words often may grow to dislike language altogether or only use harsh, tough words.

Make a point of providing your child with a full and accurate vocabulary, instead of limiting it to generalities. For example, when your child spots a dog, avoid general observations like, "Yes, there's a dog." Instead say, "Yes, that dog is an Irish Setter."

Encourage use of complete sentences. If your child says, "We go to the store," *gently* redirect him by saying, "Yes, we are going to the store," and encourage him to repeat the sentence correctly. Do not, however, correct him in front of others; children are as sensitive to this as adults are.

*Learning to read is based on good listening and talking skills, as well as good memory, and having lots of experiences.* Help your child look carefully, listen carefully and remember well. This will boost your child's chances of learning to read well in school.

Certainly the most important thing you can do to prepare your child for reading readiness is to read to him *everyday.* Only five minutes a day will make such a difference in his school readiness. Kindergarten and first grade teachers can usually tell early on which children have been exposed to books and read to regularly and those who have not.

Encourage your child to sit and turn pages and tell you the stories in picture books. Treat books as a special treasure. Let your child see you reading often.

The following suggested list of stories is intended to be a general guide of classic literature. They are all available at your local library. If you can't find a particular story, ask your librarian to locate it for you. (For a more contemporary list of childrens' literature see Chapter 8, which divides the book list into subjects relevant to children.)

### Classic Stories to Share with Your Child

Anansi Rides Tiger
Chicken Little
Cinderella
Goldilocks and the Three Bears
Jack and the Beanstalk
The Little Red Hen
Little Red Riding Hood
Medio Pollito
Peter Rabbit
The Pied Piper of Hamelin
Pinocchio
The Princess and the Pea
Puss-in-Boots
Rapunzel
Rumpelstiltskin

Sleeping Beauty
Snow White
The Three Little Pigs
The Ugly Duckling

## READING READINESS

---

### KEY TO SOUND–LETTER CORRESPONDENCE

/m/
Throughout this section a letter inside diagonal lines refers to its *sound* when it starts a word. For instance it refers to the initial sound of the spoken word /man/, a brief "mmm" sound without any vowel following.

*m*
All italicized letters refer to the printed form of the letter and children should be taught to pronounce their sound names, not their alphabet names. (Later in this chapter you will see how to teach children to respond to the printed letter *m* by its sound /m/.)

---

### A Reading Readiness Checklist

Following is an overview of all the reading readiness skills, divided according to age groups. This particular breakdown shows that each major building block rests on the completion of the previous one and does not suggest the exact age at which children should start to develop certain skills.

Three year olds should be encouraged to develop their abilities:

- to listen
- to expand their speaking vocabularies
- to concentrate (focusing on a task, shutting out distracting stimuli)
- to observe, e.g., to select a given object in a picture
- to follow directions
- to develop eye-hand coordination, e.g., to guide a pencil
- to follow a prescribed direction, learning left to right progression

Three and a half to four year olds should be encouraged to develop their abilities:

- to understand sequence (certain things occur in a certain order)
- to classify (these blocks are big and those are small)
- to develop fine auditory discrimination, specifically to identify initial (beginning) sounds of spoken words

Four to four and a half year olds should be encouraged to develop their abilities:

- to understand sound-letter correspondence
- to develop fine visual discrimination, specifically to identify letters

Reading is generally agreed to be *the* single most important skill a child can possess. It is the one that is taught earliest and continued longest. What is often overlooked is that teaching children to read is fascinating for teachers as well as parents, and not that difficult. The crux of the problem is to find ways of teaching that will capitalize on the child's natural interest.

## Don't Teach The ABCs

Psychologists agree that basically two kinds of learning exist: learning through understanding and learning through memorizing. Learning through understanding is a challenge to children's intelligence; learning through memorizing is merely a demand on their memories. Children are excited when they are able to figure out a problem on their own. Children do not enjoy memorizing ready-made answers. They prefer to learn when they are active participants. Understanding how something works produces a feeling of achievement in children.

The most important reading readiness skill is the ability to identify letters by their sound names. Children should never be given the job of memorizing the alphabet, which at this stage is simply a meaningless exercise; rather they should be allowed to discover the letters in their natural, intelligible relationship to the sound heard in words. In this way children learn to use inductive reasoning, an indispensable tool for all future learning.

A whole generation of teachers and parents brought up on the ABC song may well ask, "Why not teach the ABCs? Four year olds are so proud when they can recite the ABCs." Knowing the alphabet is an achievement that most children enjoy, but as we shall see, knowing the letter names can be a handicap in learning to read and spell. Whatever the temptation, don't teach the ABCs.

Although preschool children are fascinated by written language, telling them that the letter *m* says /em/ means nothing to them. Modern psychologists such as Piaget have shown that young children can understand a concept only when it is presented on the concrete level. Before learning letters, children must understand that a concrete object such as a mitten has a name and that this name starts with /m/ before they can grasp the idea that the sound /m/ is recorded by the symbol m. Only by moving from the concrete to the abstract can children eventually grasp that these strange squiggles on paper which we call letters, record sounds heard in words they use every day. This genuine insight into the relationship between the concrete and the abstract, between sound and symbol, is crucial. True understanding of symbolic abstractions, in contrast to rote knowledge of the ABCs, represents a gigantic step forward in children's intellectual development.

There is another even stronger reason not to teach the ABCs. Personal experience has shown me repeatedly that knowing the alphabet names can be a handicap to children. When reading the word *dog* for the first time, children should be able to sound out the word, /dog/, and realize what it means: "a dog." But they can sound out the word only if they know the sound names of the letters. Merely naming the letters, /dee/ /oh/ /gee/, does not able them to arrive at the pronunciation /dog/.

Most four and five year olds readily accept the explanation that every letter has two names, a sound name and an alphabet name, which are pronounced differently. For example, when we pronounce the word *fan*, we hear that it starts with an /f/ sound. That is what we call the sound name of the letter; we hear only the pure consonant, not a vowel sound attached to it. The alphabet name /ef/ has a completely different sound. Children readily accept the suggestion that learning the sound names of the letters is what we need when learning to read and spell. They enjoy the idea that letters, just like people, have two names: the sound names are their "first names" and the alphabet names are their "last names." They are amused by the analogy that letters, like children should be called by their first names and not by their last names.

Adults are harder to convince of this priority. Perhaps they are so accustomed to using only alphabet names that they see this knowledge of the ABCs as more useful than it is. They see the alphabet as a lesson in memorization which, like counting, should simply be taught.

It is usually difficult for grown-ups to empathize with just what learning to read means to a child. We recognize familiar words instantly, without remembering how once, long ago, we had to decipher them. Just as a jumble of unrecognizable symbols looks impossible for you to interpret, the printed pages of a book evoke the same feelings of frustration and bewilderment in a young child.

Jeff, a remedial student, came across the word *on* in his book. He kept staring at the word and saying /oh/ /en/. But saying /oh/ /en/ did not help him decode this simple word. Systematically, *he had to unlearn using the alphabet names of the letters before he could learn to read using a decoding process.*

Luther, a first grade remedial pupil, had been taught only the alphabet names of the letters in school. When he was confronted with a word he did not know, he said helplessly, "/Double u/ /ee/ ? /Double u/ /ee/ ? Which word is it?" Knowing the *sound* name of *w* might well have been a sufficient clue for him to be able to decode the simple word *we*.

Even the mature reader does not use the alphabet names of the letters in reading. Let us assume that you come across a word you do not know in a newspaper. In such a case would you say to yourself, "/aitch/ /oh/ /em/ /oh/ /tee/ /ay/ /ex/ /eye/ /ess/"? Not likely. Instead you sound out the word, "/ho/ /mo/ /tax/ /is/." Knowledge of the alphabet is needed only for looking up words in a dictionary. That skill, properly introduced in the third grade, is facilitated by knowing the sequence of the alphabet.

In contrast, children who know the sound names of the letters and who are given insight into the structure of words possess a basic tool for figuring out a great many words on their own. Examples of this transfer have occurred in many first grades, with children ranging in ability from slow to very bright. These children were able to read words like *has, mad, sad,* and *ran* on their own before they were taught these words.

Knowing the sound names of the letters is equally effective when it comes to spelling. If spelling is taught not through memorization but through analysis and understanding of the structure of words, then knowledge of the alphabet names again proves to be not only wasteful, but also detrimental to learning.

The roots of spelling, like those of reading, lie in spoken language. Children who have mastered sound letter correspondence do not need to place an extra burden on their memories by learning to spell by memorizing an unrelated sequence of letters. They know how to spell the word *hat* because they listen to themselves say /h/ /a/ /t/. They should not be expected to produce an automatic response to the word's alphabet names because they do not **hear** /aitch/ /ay/ /tee/. The word *hat* furthermore, is a linguistically regular word; they can clearly hear the individual sounds. They can then record these sounds naturally and logically by their letters, *provided they know the sound names of the letters.*

In this instance, it is *adults* who have to unlearn. Adults have to free themselves from the traditional concept that learning to spell requires being able to recite the alphabet names. We should not accept such a narrow definition of spelling. Too many children are taught to spell by memorizing the sequence of letter names: /jay/ /yoo/ /em/ /pee/ spells *jump.* Children who learn to spell this way have to remember the sequence of hundreds of letter names as if they were many different telephone numbers. Children who are taught spelling this way miss out on the exciting discovery that spelling, like reading, has as its base spoken language and is a logical recording of sounds heard in the spoken word.

Thinking ahead to the time when children will be learning other languages, there is another advantage to knowing the sound names of the letters: this knowledge provides children with a key not only to learning to read and spell in English but also in many foreign languages. For example, knowing that *f* says /f/ helps them in sounding out not only *father* but also *frère, fuente,* and *Frau* in French, Spanish, and German, respectively. Merely knowing that the letter says /ef/ is of no use in learning to read and spell in any language.

Ideally, letters should be taught as recorded *sounds* of spoken words, for speech precedes reading. The sound must be taught first; its transfer to an abstract symbol is a second step.

### Learning the Sounds Letters Make

Discovering the sound names of each letter is a learning process that makes sense to children. The first step involves identifying the beginning sounds. What is the first sound you hear when I say *mitten?* You hear /m/, not /em/. The first sound in *fan* is /f/ not /ef/. Only when this skill is acquired, should the children learn to record a sound they hear by its corresponding letter. If the spoken word *mask* is represented by a picture of a mask with the letter *m* superimposed upon it, children can learn to infer that the letter represents the beginning sound of *mask* which is /m/. *Learning letters through deductive reasoning, a form of self-teaching in fact, has more impact than if teachers or parents give the abstractions.*

It is therefore important to resist the temptation to start the introduction of letters by pointing to a printed letter and telling the children the alphabet name of the letter. Instead begin with spoken words and help children discover that every word they speak has an initial (or beginning) sound. After they can identify all the letters by their sound names, and only after this, do you have the option of teaching the ABCs. Children need these in order to learn the conventional grown-up way of identifying letters, not because the names serve any real function in learning to read and spell. Children who have good inventory memories learn the "last names" of the letters easily, and at that point the alphabet names of the letters do not interfere with reading and spelling.

## Learning Difficulties

Some children, however, have poor inventory memories, and they have difficulty learning the correspondence between each letter and its sound name. Some children have difficulty with intrasensory transfer. It is hard for them to hear /m/ then point to the visual form *m*. These children should not be introduced to a second auditory form of each letter, especially since they have to learn a second *visual* form of each letter (the capital) to be able to read sentences and proper names. It is essential that children with any of these learning difficulties not be burdened with learning the alphabet names of any of the letters at a time when such knowledge is ornamental rather than functional. In these cases it is always advisable to postpone the teaching of the ABCs.

## When to Introduce Sounds and Letters

In a good learning environment, most four and a half year olds and even four year olds, for that matter, have mastered all the necessary readiness skills and have matured to a point that they can understand sound-letter correspondence. At this age they also show an avid interest in written language.

In kindergarten, at the latest, children should start on games that let them discover sounds and letters. Natural readers should not wait beyond five, for they easily pass the critical period. Neither should children with poor visual discrimination or perceptual problems start after five. *They need at least one full year to learn some of the letters, and they should learn them* **before** *they enter first grade, as slowly as they need to.* The number of letters they learn is not as crucial as their understanding of the relationship between sounds and letters.

## Teaching Children to Write Letters

In Figure 4.1 you will see the procedure for teaching your child to write letters. You will be teaching them lowercase letters only. Why? We do not use capital letters in writing except at the beginning of a proper name or the beginning of the first word in a sentence. Thus the letters children write most often will be lowercase.

Many children who are taught both capital letters and lowercase letters *simultaneously,* cannot remember which is which and become confused and frustrated.

After the lowercase alphabet has been mastered, it is appropriate to introduce the capital alphabet (see Figure 4.2).

The arguments against teaching capital letters before lowercase letters and against using the ABCs will make sense to you if you realize that as an adult, you do not usually write words in capital letters. Nor do you make use of the ABCs in reading. So why teach them to children who are just venturing into reading and writing? It will only conflict with their learning.

### Sequence of Letters

Figure 4.1 shows how to start writing each letter by accentuating the starting point and the sequence in which to teach the letters. Because the traditional alphabetical sequence is not used, children will not fall into the habit of blindly reciting the ABCs. The sequence of letters was chosen on the basis of ease in auditory discrimination. The /m/, /f/, /l/, and /a/ are the first four letters taught because children can easily distinguish their sounds. In contrast, /m/ and /n/, which are adjacent in the alphabet, sound similar and are harder to distinguish; therefore, they should be separated by several other letters when teaching them.

It is very important that you watch your child and teach him the proper procedure for each letter, for once he learns to write a letter incorrectly, it is **very difficult** for him to *unlearn* the way he has grown accustomed to and relearn it the correct way.

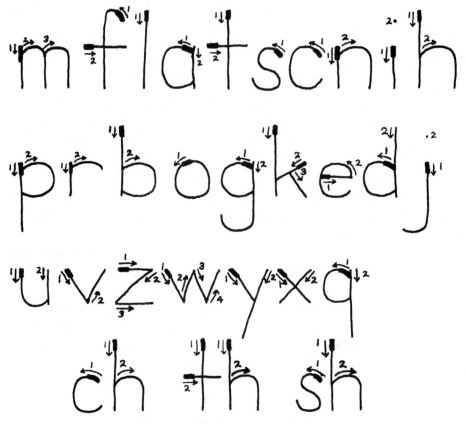

Figure 4.1. The lower-case alphabet.

## Teaching Your Child to Write His Name

Most children show a desire to learn to write their names around the ages of three or four. Many children come to kindergarten and first grade printing their name in all capital letters like this, CHARLES. This is a habit that is incredibly hard to break, so when teaching your child to write his name, print it neatly with the first letter being a capital and the letters that follow in lower case, like this, Charles. First ask your child to trace the letters with his finger, making sure he starts with the first letter and traces them in order. If left to his own devices, he will often start with the *last* letter of his name and trace it backwards. This is another habit that is hard to break. After he traces his name with his finger, watch him trace over it with a pencil or crayon. For practice, you can make several

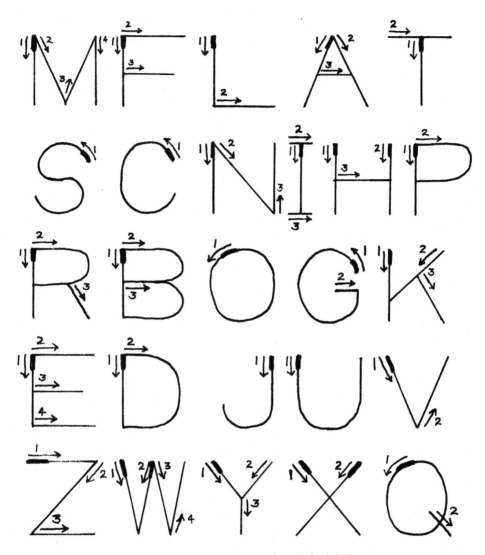

Figure 4.2. The upper-case (or capital) alphabet.

dotted outlines of his name for him to practice. Watch him until you are satisfied that he understands to begin with the *first* letter of his name and proceed in order to the *last* letter of his name.

Don't expect perfect results immediately. Handwriting is a skill that takes fine motor control that many children do not possess until the latter part of their fourth or fifth year. Praise your child, regardless of the results, and remember that it takes lots of practice and patience to learn to write. Also, if your child has a long name, such as Christopher or

Elizabeth, you should not expect them to *master* writing their name until they are five or five-and-a-half years of age. But exposure is the goal here, not perfection. If your young child can *recognize* his name when he sees it written on something, then he is doing well. Below are the norms for name and letter writing as well as the norms for writing numbers. These were established by the Gesell Institute.

## Norms for Writing Name and Letters

41/2 years:  Prints one or two recognizable letters.
  5 years:  Prints first name.
51/2 years:  Prints first name and first letter of last name.
  6 years:  Prints first and last names (girls).
61/2 years:  Prints first and last names (boys).

## Norms for Writing Numbers

4 years:  Understanding of the written symbols is just beginning. Some attempt at random numbers is made by a few at this age. Numbers made are large, and only a few are attempted.

41/2 years:  The numbers from 1 to 4 are tried by many, and many can make one or two recognizable numbers. Numbers are large and may be reversed in position. They are placed at random on the page.

5 years:  Some can make numbers up to 5. However, many confuse letters and numbers. Others make a series of vertical strokes to represent numbers. If they can write in sequence, they may omit some. Some are beginning to place their numbers in a horizontal line, though many continue to place them at random. Numbers are large (1/2 to 2 inches).

51/2 years:  Many can now write numbers from 1 to 11 or even higher. Most organize in a horizontal line. A sizable number at this age reverse numbers. Size of numbers is still large.

6 years:  Now the ability to write to 20 is close to a normative level. Double numbers may be reversed, with 20 usually being written as 02. Numbers are organized in a horizontal position.

## Letter Picture Cards

Each letter is first introduced with its letter picture card (see Figure 4.3). This is the single most important teaching device throughout the process of learning letters. The device of a letter picture makes learning each letter meaningful to children. Each letter is embedded in its picture. As children say the name of that picture, they identify its beginning sound and then can deduce what the letter on top of the picture says. Using the spoken word as a starting point creates a meaningful relationship between sound and letter.

The letter picture card is a self-teaching device. If children are unsure about a letter, all they have to do is find its letter picture card and say its name. By identifying its initial sound, they find the sound name of the letter.

## Games That Develop Sound-Letter Knowledge

The following is a list of games to help children understand sound-letter correspondence; they can be adapted to any letter or letters. We will start out with these four: *m, f, l,* and *a.* When children have mastered them, prepare for the next four (see end of chapter for letter sequence). To play these games, you need to do the following three things:

1. To make your own letter picture cards, choose a picture whose name starts with the sound you want to teach. Let's say you have drawn or cut out a picture of a mitten: paste it on a 5″ × 8″ index card. Then write with a blue magic marker a lowercase *m* on top of the picture, 1¼″ tall. The picture should be in outline form, preferably in black, so the letter stands out in the foreground (as shown in Figure 4.3).

As you prepare letter picture cards for subsequent letters, keep in mind that there is a difference in height between letters. Use these sizes:

1¼″ : m a s c n i r o e u v w x z
1¾″ : p g j q y
2″    : f l t h b k d

2. Collect objects or toys whose names start with the sounds you are going to teach your child. At the end of this chapter you will also find suggestions for which toys, pictures, or objects to use.

3. To prepare for card games, make a set of picture cards. Cut a number of 3″ × 5″ index cards in half. Look for similar sized, realistic

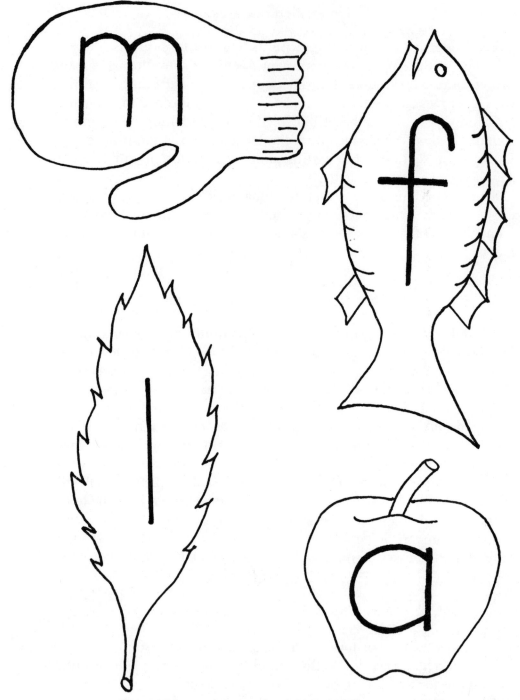

Figure 4.3. Letter picture cards, used in teaching the letter sounds.

pictures in catalogs and magazines and paste one picture on each half of the index card. (Your child's favorite cartoon or action figure may work well also.) You need five different pictures for every sound you are going to teach.

In addition, you need to write five plain letters on the same size card (one half of a 3″ × 5″ index card) to correspond to the five pictures you have selected for each letter. For instance, write five *m*s for the five *m* pictures, such as Mickey Mouse, mail carrier, mirror, mop, and mitten. Use the same size as you did for the letter picture cards. Always write the vowels in red and the consonants in blue.

### Introducing the Letter M

Put the letter picture card for *m* before the child, who identifies the picture as a mitten. Now slowly tracing the blue lines of the letter with your finger, explain that these lines form the letter that says /m/, the first sound in mitten. Let the children trace the letter with their fingers. Be sure they start at the top of the letter and proceed to trace it in the correct direction, from left to right.

### Activity 1. Pick Out The Correct Toys

Place the letter picture card for *m* upright in front of your child. Prop it up between two blocks or small boxes. Set up on a nearby chair or table your collection of toys whose names begin with the sounds /m/, /l/, and /f/. Ask a child to pick out only those toys that start with /m/ and to place them in front of the letter picture card for *m*. It is possible that your child learned the alphabet name of the letters somewhere. When they now see the letter *m*, they'll call it /em/. You don't have to say, "This is wrong." Just remind them to listen to the sound they hear. Children relearn rather quickly to give the sound name of the letter, and their knowledge of the alphabet will fade into its appropriate place. If children are able to play this game of picking out the correct toys, you can now go on to the Letter-Tracing Game.

### Activity 2. Letter-Tracing Game with One Letter

*Preparation:* Prepare sheets of paper on which you write the *m*s in dots. Draw a heavy line to indicate where children should start each letter.
*How to play:* Now explain, "If I say a word that starts with /m/ like

*mitten,* you may trace one *m.* If I say another word, like *daddy* or *school,* you must not move your pencil. Since these words do not start with /m/, you cannot trace an *m.*"

For proper development of the readiness skills, it is important that children do not trace the *m*s unless you are supervising them.

Children who have very little spatial orientation or a marked tendency toward reversals will not consistently trace the *m*s correctly. Long, hard experience has proven that from the very first tracing of a letter, children must learn to trace or write it correctly, starting at the top and proceeding in the prescribed direction. In spite of the heavy starting line indicating which way the letters go, children who lack a sense of direction frequently trace letters incorrectly or backwards. *More harm is done if a child practices tracing the wrong way than if the child never practices it at all.*

This game is most effective in helping children identify each new letter. As simple as it sounds, young children really enjoy this game.

### Activity 3. The Folder Game with Initial Sounds

*Preparation:* Paste two pockets side by side on a manila folder. Write *m* on one pocket and *f* on the other. Place a stack of picture cards with pictures of objects that begin with /m/ or /f/ face down in front of your child.

*How to play:* As children turn up a picture, they have to put it in the correct pocket.

*Variation:* As children learn more letters, use a folder with five handmade pockets. Write one letter to be mastered on each pocket.

### Activity 4. Sorting Game with Envelopes

*Preparation:* For this game for a child to play alone, take an ordinary manila folder and use masking tape to make a pocket inside it. On the pocket, tape one of the big *m*s that you have made. Take small envelopes and put a picture in each envelope. Use some pictures of things that start with /m/ and some that do not.

*How to play:* Give the envelopes to your child and ask her to open one envelope at a time. If the picture inside the envelope starts with /m/, she can place the envelope in the pocket; if not, she should discard it in a pile to the left.

When a child knows the letter *m* reasonably well and is eager to go ahead, introduce your letter picture for /f/, following the same procedure you did for /m/. Ask the child to identify the picture of the fish and give you the beginning sound. Always make sure that the child knows the meaning of each word studied. Trace the blue lines of the *f* with your finger, explaining that since this is a *fish,* whose name starts with /f/, the blue lines form the letter *f.*

From here on, go very slowly, depending on the individual child. Some children find it very difficult to identify *m* and *f* without their letter pictures. If you feel that a child is not ready for more letters, you can play the following games with this child.

Always place the letter pictures, in this case *m* and *f,* first in front of, later in back of, the children so they can easily check for themselves what the letters say whenever they need to.

The letter pictures are a self-corrective tool, very much like a dictionary. If children have forgotten the sound of a given letter, they look it up in the set of letter pictures. Once they have located the letter picture, they say out loud the name of the letter picture and listen to its first sound. They hear themselves say the sound and thus, without your help, are able to deduce the sound name of the letter. They develop a sense of security knowing that they can look up a letter in case of uncertainty or to correct an error. They do not feel the burden of having to memorize a letter, nor are they subjected to the diminishing experience of being told that they are wrong or "you made a mistake." Please avoid saying this at all costs. If you feel you must correct your child say, "Let's try doing it this way."

### Activity 5. Filing Pictures Under Correct Letters

*Preparation:* Children enjoy having a filing box. You can buy an inexpensive one that will hold 3″ × 5″ index cards, or you can make one simply out of an old shoe box. Put tabs on top of some index cards, which will then serve as dividers. On each tab write one of the letters your child knows.

*How to play:* Give children an old magazine or mail catalog. Ask them to look for pictures whose names have beginning sounds corresponding to those letters. They cut out each picture, paste it on an index card, then file it behind the proper letter.

## Activity 6. Grab Bag Game

*How to play:* Have your child close her eyes and pick one toy from a bag of toys. After she says the name of the toy, have her put it in front of the correct letter picture card. After a while, replace these letter picture cards by index cards bearing only the letters.

*Variation:* Prepare sheets of paper with dotted *m*s and *f*s. A child picks out a toy and traces one *m* if its name starts with /m/, or traces one *f* if its name starts with /f/. If the name of the toy begins with any other letter, the child should identify its beginning sound even though there is no corresponding letter to trace. To make the game more interesting, the two of you can each guess beforehand which line will win, the *m*s or the *f*s.

## Activity 7. Matching Game

*Preparation:* Cut unlined 3″ × 5″ index cards in half. Write one *m* on each of five cards, and write one *f* on each of five cards. Help your child find and cut out five pictures that start with /m/ and five pictures that start with /f/, or you may draw them. Paste each picture on half an index card.

*How to play:* Now combine the letter cards and picture cards, shuffle them, and place them face down. Take turns picking up one card. The picture cards should go to the right of the table and the letter cards to the left. When a letter and a picture card match, claim a match. The player who claims the most matched pairs wins.

*Variation:* Show your child how to play a sorting game by himself as he matches a picture with the corresponding letter card, and then turns the matched pair over.

## Letter Reversals

Almost all children commonly reverse *b* and *d*, *p* and *q*, and *g* and *p* since they "look alike" for a very long time. If your child has forgotten the name or shape of any of these letters have them look it up and check it with the letter picture card. Try not to supply the answer. If your child rechecks the name with its letter picture card, they are rewarded with the confidence that they can figure out each letter's sound on their own.

In persistent cases of *b* and *d* reversal, an easy technique you can use is to draw a large, clear *b* on a sheet of paper and hang it on the wall. The *b* has a "belly."

Your child could also draw or paste on construction paper pictures of objects whose names start with /b/. In a different room hang a piece of paper with the letter *d,* but alter its configuration so that it is not as heavily lined as the *b* and also serves to remind the child of its letter picture, the duck.

Experience has taught me that many children take a disproportionately long time to learn the first four to six letters. As they get the hang of it, they learn each successive letter faster.

In teaching capital letters, introduce four capital letters at a time, using the sequence of letters outlined in Figure 4.2. Print each letter on one-half of a 3″ × 5″ index card. Place these letters under the corresponding picture cards. Then play the letter tracing game.

## When Not to Increase Play Time

Don't increase the play time you spend with your child just because the child is having difficulty learning a letter. You must be patient. *Any concern or pressure defeats the real goal of helping children gain a feeling of competence in an area of difficulty.*

If at any time you find yourself saying "No, that is wrong!" Or either one of you begins to feel frustrated, please, for the sake of your child, stop. You don't want your child to associate letters and learning with negative, defeatist feelings.

Once the children have learned two letters, they have learned far more than just two letters. They have understood two facts: first, letters record sounds; and second, letters face a definite direction and have to be formed in a specific way. Their understanding that letters record sounds is the important result of your teaching, NOT the number of letters they know. This insight is crucial for their success in learning to read.

## Discovering How to Read

When a child is discovering how to read, he goes through the process of learning a set of rules and acquiring a sense of order. Those first encounters are a lesson about the inconsistency and unreliability of language. Depending on a child's nature, this serves as either an additional challenge and a source of intrigue, or as a frustration so great that he throws down his book and returns to his game. But that doesn't mean he's a lost cause or an indifferent student. It only means he'd rather play with something else.

This will likely continue for an uncomfortable amount of time. But in the end, it is unlikely to be any one thing—blocks or alphabet puzzles or "Sesame Street" jingles or even the presence of an inspired teacher—that brings about a child's reading breakthrough. You can foster a climate of learning and make it fun. You can fill your home with books and children's magazines and follow every step mentioned in this book. But a child learns to read when *he* is ready. If he isn't, you can sound out *cat* 30 times a day and still he may look at the word and say *dog*. When he is ready, he may just open *The Cat in the Hat* and read right through the first ten pages.

Of all the landmarks in a child's life—the first smile, the first haircut, the first day of school—few seem more significant than the moment when the ability to read kicks in. It's a gradual process, of course, preceded by years spent learning the letters and their sounds, looking at books, manipulating learning games. But for a lot of children, there is a sudden and thrilling instant when everything seems to click. One day letters on a page are a frustrating jumble; the next day the fog lifts. And there it is: first a word, then a sentence, and then a complete thought.

Interesting to note: Singer and Singer report that the best predictors of good reading comprehension in primary school children are minimal TV viewing during the preschool period, nonphysical discipline, a curious resourceful mother, and an orderly household routine.

## Sequence of Letters and Suggested Pictures for Each Letter

| | |
|---|---|
| /m/ | magnet, mirror, marble, milk bottle, mop, mailbox, monkey, mouse, mitten, magazine, matches, mask |
| /f/ | feather, fork, football, fan, fish, fishing rod, finger |
| /l/ | lemon, lion, lamb, ladder, lipstick, loaf, lid, letter, lime, leaf, lollipop, lamp, leopard, lettuce |
| /a/ | ax, anchor, ant, apple, ambulance, astronaut |
| /t/ | telephone, towel, toothbrush, tie, tent, tomato, teapot, turtle, top, tiger, table, toothpaste, turkey |
| /s/ | sandwich, saw, sailboat, soap, salt, seal, sock, sun |
| initial /k/ spelled *c* | cup, cap, candle, curtain, carrot, cake, camel, cat, cane, can, cape, cookie, candy, corn, comb |
| /n/ | nest, net, needle, napkin, nut, nail, nurse, numerals, newspaper, necktie, note, nickel |

| | |
|---|---|
| /i/ | igloo, inch, Indian, ink, insect |
| /h/ | hat, hose, hammer, hen, hanger, heart, house, horse, horn, handbag, helicopter, hand, hoe |
| /p/ | paper, perfume, pizza, penny, pin, pail, peacock, pie, puppet, pipe, pelican, paintbrush |
| /r/ | raccoon, raisin, ribbon, radio, rope, rake, radish, robot, rocket, rose, rooster, ring |
| /b/ | beads, bicycle, box, belt, bat, boot, ball, bell, balloon, book, buckle, bee, bib, basket, bowl |
| /o/ | olive, ostrich, otter, ox, orchid, octopus, orange |
| /g/ | gum, garage, golf club, guitar, goose, gift |
| initial /k/ spelled *k* | kangaroo, key, kerchief, king, kite, kettle, kitten |
| /e/ | egg, eggplant, elf, envelope, Eskimo, elephant |
| /d/ | doctor, dish, daisy, duck, doughnut, dime, domino |
| /j/ | jacket, jump rope, jacks, jam, jar |
| /u/ | umpire, umbrella, Uncle Sam |
| /v/ | vinegar, vase, violin, violet, vest, valentine |
| /z/ | zebra, zoo, zinnia, zero, zipper |
| /w/ | wagon, wigwam, windmill, wallet, watermelon, wishbone, web, witch |
| /y/ | yo-yo, yak, yarn, yardstick, yolk |
| /q/ | quail, quilt, queen, question mark, quarter (coin), quotes |
| /ch/ | chick, chocolate, chimney, church, cherries, chipmunk, chain, cheese, checkers |
| /th/ | thistle, thermometer, thimble, thorn |
| /sh/ | sheep, shovel, ship, shoe, shell, shirt |

Consider the fact that when you choose some of the more unusual words, you are increasing your child's vocabulary.

## A Child's First Word List

Following is a list of the most frequently used words in most children's literature.

| | | | | |
|---|---|---|---|---|
| a | day | him | oh | they |
| all | did | home | old | this |
| am | do | hot | on | three |
| an | dog | house | one | to |
| and | down | how | or | too |
| any | eat | I | out | top |
| are | end | if | pig | two |
| as | fat | I'll | play | up |
| ask | find | in | put | us |
| at | fish | into | ran | walk |
| ate | fly | is | red | was |
| away | for | it | ride | we |
| be | funny | jump | run | well |
| bed | get | let | sad | will |

| | | | | |
|---|---|---|---|---|
| big | girl | like | said | with |
| black | give | look | saw | woman |
| blue | go | made | say | work |
| book | going | make | see | yellow |
| boy | good | man | she | yes |
| brown | got | many | sit | you |
| bus | had | me | slow | |
| but | has | mouse | so | |
| by | hat | must | stop | |
| call | have | my | sun | |
| came | he | new | tell | |
| can | help | no | that | |
| car | hen | not | the | |
| come | her | now | them | |
| cry | here | of | then | |

## Invented Spelling

As children become writers, they invent spellings for words they want to use. Invented spelling is what we call children's misspellings before they learn all the rules adults use to spell. Children's errors give us a window on what they know. If a child spells dinosaur "dnsr" we see that he is using beginning sounds heavily and is relying on the consonant sounds instead of vowels. *This is exactly what he should be doing at his developmental stage.*

Invented spelling does *not* interfere with children's ability to spell correctly later. There are lots of advantages for the child who uses invented spelling. Here are some:

- Encourages children to figure out the alphabet
- Makes children independent as writers; they don't have to ask others how to spell words; it frees them from depending on others
- Encourages children to write longer, more colorful stories because they can write anything they can say. Writing more equals writing better.
- They are not limited to writing only the words they know how to read.
- Encourages children to take responsibility for their own learning and puts them in control of what they write and how they write it.
- Provides extensive practice in phonics; children practice their sounds as they write using letters to represent the sounds they hear in words.

Here is a sample from a five year old using invented spelling:

I love riten becaes I wat to lrn to red.

(Translation: I love writing because I want to learn to read.)

Many parents are concerned that their children will not eventually learn to spell correctly. Let me assure you: *invented spelling is a developmental step; children go on to learn to spell even better than they would if they had not been allowed to take these beginning steps.* Invented spelling frees them from being afraid to write because "I don't know how to spell that word."

Don't be overly concerned when your budding writer misspells every word. Resist the temptation to correct everything and encourage him to keep writing. If his writing is met with, "Oh, that's good, but you misspelled these words," he will surely not write as much as the child who is met with nothing but praise for his efforts. Your child will be given a spelling list to memorize soon enough, so relax and enjoy the creative writing efforts of your child.

# Chapter 5

# LEARNING ACTIVITIES

## PLACES TO GO

Virtually every place you go with your child can be turned into a learning experience. By asking simple questions designed to get your child to think and observe, and by introducing the vocabulary native to the particular environment you happen to be in, you can expand your child's mind and help her reach her full potential.

### The Library

September is National Library Card Sign-Up Month. Think about the benefits your children can receive from their local library. There are books, of course, but many libraries also offer records, tapes, videocassettes, games, puzzles, and toys. Some libraries run movies for children or arrange storytelling sessions; some hold puppet shows. While you are at the library, introduce new vocabulary words like *card catalog, information,* and *reference* to your child. Give your children the gift of discovery and fun by giving them a library card.

### The Zoo

In this increasingly urban society, the opportunities for our children to learn about and appreciate nature grow fewer by the decade. One way to stimulate your child's interest in nature is to plan a trip to the zoo.

Write to the zoo before your visit to obtain a map or a brochure so you can plan which sites to see. The animals are most active at feeding time, so you may want to get a schedule of these times. If you visit during the off season, there are less crowds and you may even find a zookeeper who has some time to talk to you. It is good experience for children to meet people from as many different walks of life as possible.

Explain the rules of proper behavior to your children. Impress upon your children that they will be looking at *wild animals;* these animals may seem tame and friendly, but they can bite and scratch quickly and fiercely.

A certain frenzy overtakes many zoo visitors. They run from exhibit to exhibit "seeing everything" but actually experiencing and learning nothing. To help your children get the most from their visit, take your time and let them linger over their favorite animal.

Ask your child thought-provoking questions: Which elephant seems to be the boss? Do they seem to have individual personalities? Also discuss why animals have different types of feet, beaks, and body coverings and what these characteristics say about the animals' diets, habits, and native regions.

Introduce new vocabulary such as *habitat, camouflage, tame* versus *wild, extinct, endangered species, desert,* and *tropical forest.*

A zoo environment provides an ideal environment for young children to apply observation skills. How are the four tigers the same? How are they different?

Observe the habitats. Many zoos have their own nurseries and grow plants that are found in the animals' natural habitats. Which kinds of plants and trees are found in each exhibit? Are they sources of camouflage? food? Are they native to deserts? mountains? tropical forests?

Discuss ecology. By the year 2000, approximately 600,000 species of plants and animals may be extinct. Your children or grandchildren may be the last generation to see many animals alive. To learn more about endangered species, write to the National Audubon Society at 950 Third Avenue, New York, New York 10022, or visit your local library.

### Historic Places

It seems trips with young children to historic sites can either stimulate a lasting interest in history, or kill it. Some forethought and careful planning can make a real difference. Here are some tips:

- Match visits to children's interests. Your children will enjoy exploring old boats, airplanes or other transportation exhibits.
- Read and discuss stories about the historic places prior to your visit emphasizing the "human factor." Reading the story of the exhibit gives the visit a context.

- Famous or familiar names are a good stimulus. It's more satisfying to take children places that feature people they have heard about.
- Seek out some of the folk festivals that take place, where children can participate in traditional crafts or perhaps dress up in period garb.
- Give high priority to "hands on" historic sites and museums.
- Focus on food. Children will enjoy and remember a visit to a colonial kitchen if they also taste a bit of corn bread topped with maple syrup.
- Choose places that have short but informative orientation films. Then select those attractions most likely to appeal to your children. Don't feel like you have to see every attraction at one site.
- Balance the "history time" with some free play time.
- Take lots of pictures or buy postcards of the historic places you visit. The experience will be reinforced when your children use the pictures at school or to make a scrapbook. Many children enjoy collecting postcards from every place they visit.
- Prepare in advance. Most states have historical societies and tourists offices that will supply good leads.
- Take the time to select two or three new vocabulary words from the exhibit and teach them to your child.
- Summer is a great time to encourage interest in geography. The U.S. Department of Education has a wonderful 25-page booklet called *Helping Your Child Learn Geography,* full of ways to engage children's interest, including how to explore the geography of their immediate neighborhood and how to study the weather. The booklet, which is in color, also has good maps. Send your request and 50 cents to Consumer Information Center, Department 85, Pueblo, Colorado 81009.

### The Museum

When taking young children to the museum, its best to try to choose an exhibit that can be meaningful or interesting to the child. Many large cities now have children's museums, which are usually affiliated with a large art, history, or science museum. There are also many exhibits planned specifically for children during the year. Call your local museum for a schedule.

Before your visit, check out a few books from the library on the subject presented at the museum, to share with your child. This will make the visit more meaningful and enjoyable for your child.

If the exhibit is a large one, plan to see only those parts you feel that your child would enjoy.

Ask questions about your child's opinion of what she is viewing. If it is art, discuss how different art can be and how there is no "right way" or "wrong way" in the creative world. This idea appeals to many children who often feel that they don't do things well. Discuss freedom of expression and style. Encourage your child to create a "work of art" when you return home.

New vocabulary could include *sculpture, artifacts, relics, antiques, skeleton,* and *display.*

After your visit, be sure to discuss the details of your trip and ask specific questions concerning what you saw together. This will reinforce the experience and make it more likely to be remembered a few months later.

Museums are wonderful ways to open up small minds to the wonders of the world and expand their horizons for the future.

## The Airport

Young children love to see huge airplanes take off and land. Viewing it on television cannot compare to the first hand experience of seeing a huge jet rev up its engines and take off into the blue sky. The noise, the smell, and the sight of it all are very memorable and exciting to a young child. Don't forget how the simple things in this world look to your child. What has become an ordinary experience for you is an extraordinary experience for your child.

While at the airport, use the experience as an opportunity to introduce new vocabulary such as *transportation, flight, reservation, pilot, luggage, lobby, arrival, departure,* and *exit.*

Before you leave the airport, buy a postcard to help your child remember the trip. (Don't forget to people watch and watch the luggage fall onto the *carousel.* )

When you get home, ask your child to draw a picture of what he saw at the airport.

## The Creative Arts

Take your child to a performance of mimes, dancers, story tellers and theater groups geared to young children. If you live near a large city, don't miss the opportunity to see a first class musical or opera presented by paid professionals. Such an experience for a child is usually something that sparks a lifelong interest in the subject matter, music, theater, or all of these. If the story or play being presented is a popular one, check out the book version from the library and read it to your child beforehand. He will enjoy it more if he is familiar with the story. While some of these performances may be costly, others run by nonprofit groups and high school and college performing arts clubs are usually very reasonably priced. Afterwards ask your child which part of the performance he enjoyed the most, the least, and why.

## The Grocery Store

Taking young children to the grocery store is usually not a desirable expedition but the grocery store can be a great learning experience. Use it to teach words like *frozen, sale, cheap, expensive, pharmacy, isle, deli, bakery, seafood, produce,* and *dairy.* Each time you visit the store, give your child a task such as "Count how many *red* things you can find in the store today." Or for an older child, "How many foods can you find that begin with the letter *c* ?" or "I need some apples; what sound does *apple* start with?"

Help your child to understand the different food groups such as fruits, vegetables, dairy, and grain products.

# THINGS TO DO

## Making Play Dough

Play dough is a wonderful way to keep little hands occupied while encouraging your child's creativity as well. If it is stored in an airtight container, it will keep well. Below is the recipe. Let your child watch as you add the food coloring. This can be a great opportunity to teach a simple lesson on colors.

| | |
|---|---|
| 1/2 cup of salt | 1 cup of water |
| 1 cup of flour | 1 tbsp. vegetable oil |
| 2 tbsp. cream of tartar | food coloring |

Mix salt, flour, and cream of tartar together. Add water, oil, and food coloring. Cook mixture on medium heat until dough feels right (3 to 5 minutes). Store in a plastic bag or a container with a lid.

Using red, blue, and yellow, you can also make these colors; green (mix blue and yellow), orange (mix red and yellow), purple (mix red and blue). Start with a small amount of food coloring and add accordingly or your colors will be dull.

## Baker's Clay

4 cups flour
1 1/2 cups water
1 cup salt

Mix the flour, salt, and water together and roll out as cookie dough. Cut with cookie cutters or mold your own figures. Bake at 325 until light brown.

This dough can be shaped into mushrooms, bells, Raggedy Ann dolls, letters of your child's name, or just about anything. One note of caution: If you are planning to make hanging ornaments (for Christmas, for example), be sure to make holes in the clay *before* it is baked.

After it has baked and cooled, help your child paint her creations.

## Finger Paint Recipe

| | |
|---|---|
| 1/2 cup cornstarch | 2 cups hot water |
| 1 cup cold water | 1/2 cups soap flakes or detergent |
| 1 envelope unflavored gelatin | food coloring |

Combine starch and 3/4 cup cold water. Soak gelatin in remaining 1/4 cup cold water. Stir hot water slowly into cornstarch mixture. Cook and stir over medium heat until mixture boils and is clear. Remove from heat and blend in softened gelatin. Stir in soap or detergent until dissolved. Cool, then divide into a jar for each color. Stir food coloring into mixture to desired intensity. Cover jars to store.

## Homemade Blocks

Because they have so much imagination, children love simple toys. Help them make their own blocks by covering empty cookie boxes, milk containers, formula cans, and paper towel rolls with colorful contact paper. The variety of shapes lends itself well to a number of construction projects.

## Using the Telephone

Before your child begins school, she should have some experience with the telephone. She should know how to use the phone in an emergency, and also her own home phone number and address. If she has working parents, she should memorize at least one parent's work phone number.

An easy way to teach this information to your child would be for her to hear you repeat it to her once a day for several weeks. After a few repetitions you can make a game out of it. Repeat your work number to her and say, "whose number is that?". After a while, she will be able to recite it with you. After you teach your child her phone number, make sure you review it every once in a while to ensure that she does not forget it.

Another method for teaching this information to your child is to make a tape using a tape recorder. A sample tape may sound something like this: "My name is Sara Nixon. I live at 123 White Oak Drive. My phone number is 555-1234. I can call my mom at work when I dial 555-4321." Your child will love hearing herself on the tape recorder. You can say the information first, and she can repeat it into the recorder. Use this method for teaching other necessary information to your child.

An easy way to teach your child her address is simply to say your address every time you pull your car into the driveway. "Well, here we are at 123 White Oak Drive!"

Your child should also be instructed how to use the telephone in the event of an emergency. We don't like to think about it, but you or your child's caregiver could faint, fall, or suddenly become ill. Would your child know how to use the telephone to call for help?

With assistance, preschoolers can learn how to use the phone in an emergency. One way to teach them is to make Phone Pages. For each phone number, draw seven telephone dials or button panels on the bottom half of a sheet of paper. Write in the numbers 1 through 9 and 0; with a yellow highlighter marker, color in the number to be dialed. Print the phone numbers in large bold letters above the dials. Then paste a picture of the place or person the number reaches—such as fire station or police. Use a photo of you at work for your work number. Include names and addresses in the top corners. Draw three dials for 911 if your community uses that system, and use small pictures of the service it reaches (see Figure 5.1).

Using a photograph of your house or apartment building, make a phone page for your home. Clearly print your full name and address above your telephone number and the dials or panels. Have your child practice "reading" the page to help her memorize the information for times when she is away from home, too.

Instruct your child in a calm reassuring manner about when it is necessary to use the phone pages. Have her practice dialing each phone number on a disconnected phone; she can practice announcing her full name and address so she is prepared when asked by the 911 operator. Tell your child that if she cannot reach the number she is dialing, she can bring the phone pages to a reliable neighbor for help. Seeing the phone numbers with the pictures can allow a neighbor to understand the situation with little explanation from an upset child.

## Teach Your Child to Tie Her Shoes in 5 Easy Steps

Imagine how many shoes a kindergarten teacher ties in a year. You can make her job easier if you send your child to school already knowing this task. Many children try to tie their shoes before they have the vaguest idea how to do it—and before their fine motor skills are developed enough. This can be the source of much unnecessary frustration. However, by age five, most children are ready to learn. According to Debra Morgenstern Katz, here are five simple steps a sampling of parents have used successfully.

*Step 1*—Take one shoelace in one hand, the second lace in the other, and hold both of them straight up. Then crisscross the laces over each other so that they form an X.

*Step 2*—Fold one lace over the other and pull that lace through the bottom half of the X; then pull both of the laces tight until they lie nice and flat against the shoe.

*Step 3*—Many children find that this "bunny ears" method is easier to

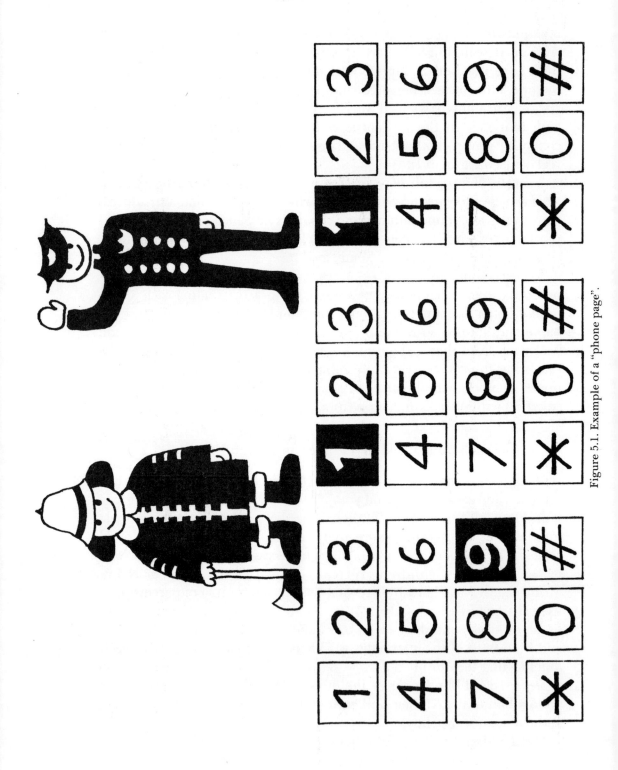

Figure 5.1. Example of a "phone page".

learn than the one loop method (the way most adults tie their shoes). Make two loops, one with each shoelace.

*Step 4* — Make an X with the loops, holding the center of the X in place with your thumb and finger. (Children may have to switch hands when they do this part.)

*Step 5* — Fold one loop over the other (as you did with the first X) and pull that loop through the bottom half of the X. Now pull both loops tight through the hole to form a bow.

Your child's practice, along with your patience, will eventually make perfect. Here are some helpful tips:

1. Don't rush it. This is a skill that takes some time to master.
2. Let your child succeed at one step before moving on to the next. Repetition is important, so each step, or even each part of the more complicated steps should be practiced for a few days.
3. Allow extra time in the mornings; once your child starts to learn, she will want to do it all by herself. By building the time into your routine, you'll avoid unnecessary frustration.
4. Use flat laces, which are easier to manipulate than round laces.
5. Make sure the laces are long enough. Beginners just don't have the dexterity to work with short laces.
6. Some children have an easier time learning on the "dress me" dolls or cloth teaching books that include shoelaces. You can find these products at most toy stores.
7. For some children, adult-size shoes and laces are easier to practice on.
8. Children develop at different rates. If some of your child's friends can tie their shoes, assure your child that she will get it soon and remind her of the skills she does have.

### Just For Fun

1. Ask your child to help you measure the ingredients to your favorite cookie recipe.
2. Read a classic book together.
3. Teach your child to play checkers, or some other simple board game.
4. Star gaze.
5. Make Jello® jigglers.
6. Cut paper dolls out of catalogs.

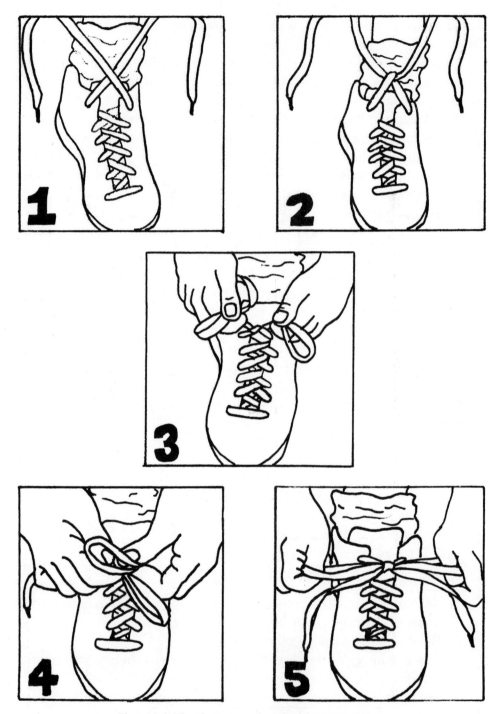

Figure 5.2. The "bunny ears" method for tying shoes.

7. Paint a flower pot and plant some seeds. Your child will love watching them grow.
8. Create a collage with rice, beans, and macaroni. After it dries, hang it proudly.
9. Using an ink pad, make finger print animals. Draw in their face, ears, arms, and legs.
10. Play classical music. Expose your child to a variety of music.
11. Make a puzzle by gluing a picture to a piece of cardboard and then cutting out puzzle shapes.
12. Dress up in old clothes.
13. Use pictures of animals, plants, the solar system, insects, and special sights in nature to create a stimulating environment in your young child's room.
14. Create a mosaic with small pieces of construction paper cut or torn into small pieces.
15. Fill the bottom of 2 liter bottles with water and use as bowling pins.
16. Make a bird feeder by rolling pine cones in peanut butter and then in bird seed.
17. Make a book using a photo album.
18. Design a stained glass window. Shave crayons onto waxed paper, cover with second sheet and place inside folded newspaper. Iron on low heat.
19. Talk about a different culture or country, check out books with pictures of the country and eat food from the country.
20. Mark your child's height on a wall and date it. She will love seeing herself grow. Explain *feet* and *inches.*
21. Make leaf and coin rubbings by placing them under a sheet of paper and coloring over them.
22. Cut apart a favorite comic strip from the Sunday news and help your child reassemble it.
23. Discuss directions: the sun rises in the east and sets in the west. Birds fly south in the winter, and north in the summer.
24. Make a mask out of a brown grocery bag.
25. Put up a map of the world. Talk about where friends and family live as well as animals of the world, or events on television.
26. Encourage your child to start a collection of rocks, seeds, stamps, postcards, bugs, or other interest. Help her label the collection.
27. Take time to observe and describe the weather each day. Keep a

daily weather chart, drawing sun, rain, clouds, to depict weather. Help your child notice different types of clouds and introduce the names for the various types of clouds (cumulus, stratus, and so on.)

28. Try some simple science at home. Pour a little vinegar in the bottom of a bottle with a narrow neck. Next put 2 teaspoons of baking soda into a balloon and quickly attach the balloon over the neck of the bottle. Watch as the balloon blows up! Help your child understand that a gas was formed when the soda combined with the vinegar.

29. Help your child rub different objects together—his hands, two rocks, and so on. Introduce the term *friction* to explain the heat that results. Explain how early fires were started using this concept.

30. Make a crystal garden. Break up several charcoal briquets into an old pie pan. Add 2 tablespoons each of salt, water, ammonia, and bluing. As the liquid evaporates, crystals will grow.

## PEOPLE TO MEET

Almost all kindergarten curriculums will do a study of people in the community. Discussed are firemen, policemen, mail carriers, veterinarians, doctors, nurses, teachers, etc., and the job-related duties of each. Think of your friends as resources and introduce your children to anyone who knows how something works. It is important to expose children to positive role models early in life. Think creatively: basket weavers, mechanics, amateur musicians and singers, and landscapers are all examples of workers you could expose your child to. If you have a friend who refinishes old furniture, or paints or draws for fun, take your child with you one day when you go for a visit. Keep your eyes open and look to see which person your child seems most interested in. Then find ways to expand on that craft or profession. Foster your child's interests.

# Chapter 6

# DISCUSS THIS BEFORE SOMEONE ELSE DOES

## DRUG PREVENTION STARTS EARLY

S ad as it may be, yes, it is necessary to discuss drugs with your young child. Kathryn R. Boyer, who conducted a study on juvenile crime in Washington D.C. in 1989 says, "We're going to have a whole generation of young kids who have fried their brains by the time they are 15." Indeed, 24 percent of fourth graders nationwide said kids their age feel pressure to try cocaine or crack, according to a poll by *Weekly Reader,* a national newspaper for schoolchildren.

Other surveys show that overall drug use among the young has actually declined in recent years, with fewer high school students smoking marijuana and snorting cocaine. But take a look at some of the criminal statistics, and it seems that while the middle class may have cut down on its intake, poor and minority children are more vulnerable than ever to the cheaper and more powerful drugs available. According to one newspaper, between 1980 and 1987 the number of juveniles arrested for coke-related (often crack) crimes more than doubled in Detroit, tripled in New York, and skyrocketed in Los Angeles—where it increased by a factor of 40. The statistics go on and on, from soaring murder rates to the number of cocaine-related hospital emergencies to the percentage of infants born each day addicted to drugs.

Of course, each and every one of us will bear the high cost of such pervasive drug use: in tax dollars, in higher insurance rates, in increased crime. Our social service agencies are overwhelmed by the drug problem, which means they have fewer resources to provide prenatal care or daycare, or to deal with child abuse, homelessness, and hunger. And the biggest cost of all, of course, is the damage done to the moral fiber of the community. Guns and murder become commonplace, as do 11-year-old drug dealers wearing beepers that sound off during math lessons in school. At bottom we're left with a sense of indifference to the lives lost to drugs.

Although crack is still primarily an inner-city problem, drug use doesn't stop at the boarders of the ghetto. We may point to the poor children hawking crack along city streets, but there are plenty of well-educated, well-mannered, well-adjusted students dealing pot and cocaine, if not always crack, in suburban junior high and high schools. The middle-class romance with getting high has not faded; according to a 1987 study funded by the U.S. Department of Health and Human Services, more than one-third of tenth-grade students have tried pot, and one out of every ten, cocaine. Today affluent, suburban parents, as well as their less well-off counterparts, see drugs threatening the lives of their children.

As young schoolchildren reach junior high school, whether they're in public or private institutions, they will see schoolmates get caught in the web of drugs that stretches into every neighborhood. And of course, the day will come when they are offered drugs. It is inevitable in a country where drugs are so available, so cheap, so seductive.

The problem for parents is that our children are confused. They receive too many mixed signals. They see that even when juveniles are caught with drugs, the authorities prefer to keep them out of jail; that with overcrowded prisons and overbooked court dockets, the threat of jail for drug possession is basically an empty sanction. Meanwhile, our political leaders resort to simplistic, foot-stomping slogans like *"Drugs Kill"* and *"Just Say No";* and while we need to send consistent, clear messages about the dangers of drugs, such slogans do nothing without real programs behind them. Until the start of the *Say No to Drugs* Campaign, American society gave no strong message to children about drugs. But the cruel truth is that *"Just Say No"* is a prime example of a lip-service program that totally lacks any real financial commitment to actually help stop drug use.

Although the slogan may be catchy and easily understood, it doesn't speak to the realities that lead people to the world of drugs. Drugs are not an isolated issue. Young people often use them as an expression of other problems: frustrations with siblings or with inattentive parents; setbacks in school; personal difficulties, such as lack of self-confidence, sense of direction, or supportive, positive role models and friends. Children with an unsure sense of identity will rely on drugs to help them separate from their parents, find a social niche, or establish intimacy with their friends. Indeed, peer pressure can never be underestimated. It is probably the sole factor that applies equally to children of all academic, social, and economic levels: the need to fit in and be cool.

The solution for parents lies in four key concepts.

*First, drug prevention starts early, when your child is a toddler—not a teenager.* By then it is too late. You can't lecture a toddler, or your preschooler for that matter, about the dangers of crack, but on the other hand, you *can* help him develop self-esteem. A child who has strong goals, strong values, and strong role models may at some point experiment with marijuana, but he is far less likely to become focused or dependent on drugs. To a confident, self-directed youngster intent on growth and achievement, drugs can be just another fact of modern life; to an aimless, unhappy one, drugs can be devastating. In this sense, drug use is symptomatic of a society producing too many people who don't know what they want to do with their lives, too many people who believe that as long as they don't get caught they can do anything they want, and too many people who have no idea of how they can work to make their dreams become a reality.

If money is the main lure of dealing drugs, then parents will have to show their children other ways to earn it. But again, what's even more important is for parents to encourage their children to realize their abilities—to show them what they can do and become if they don't waste their talents on the short-run thrill of drugs. The *Beginning Alcohol and Addictions Basic Education Studies* (BABES), a "primary prevention" program suggest the following ways to present children with positive alternatives and help children build their self-esteem:

- *Teach Choice:* Let children practice choosing things and trusting their own judgement. This helps develop the will to resist peer pressure. Even toddlers can pick which color shirt to wear. Other choices: play activities, friends to invite over, and stories to hear.
- *Listen and talk:* Ask and answer questions. Give your children your full attention. Talk with them in the car, at the table, and elsewhere around the house. Take a child's advise when you can. This greatly enhances self-esteem as well as conversational skills.
- *Set a Good Example:* Show children the importance of taking care of themselves—by turning down alcoholic drinks, not smoking, and maintaining a healthy diet yourself. Health-conscious children are less likely to try drugs.
- *Establish limits:* Set and enforce rules for health and safety. This helps your children feel safe and loved, and teaches them self-discipline. Discipline is best imparted through communication, not

coercion, and it's a good idea to let children have something to say in defining rules and responsibilities.

- *Enrich experience:* Explore new activities with your children. Whenever practical, take them on field trips to children's museums, playgrounds, stores, even to the workplace. Let them meet scientists, artists, workers in interesting fields, athletes. (See Chapter 5 for more specific suggestions.) Getting high has less attraction to children who have grown up with a wide range of early experiences.
- *Encourage expression:* Talk openly about how you feel and help your children do the same. The more children are able to handle their emotions, the less likely they may be to anesthetize themselves with narcotics.

***The second key is no lies.*** Conversations about drugs should be a regular part of discussions with children. There's simply no sense in trying to avoid the subject—children will simply get their information elsewhere. Nor should parents oversimplify the issue. While it may be a good idea to tell very young children that drugs are evil, as they become older it is smarter to discuss with them the attractive and the dangerous aspects of specific drugs. Marijuana use does not inescapably lead to the use of heroin or other hard drugs, but it is reasonable to point out that people who continually socialize with dope smokers are likely to find themselves in the company of people trying other drugs; and that because those people are their friends, or friends of friends, it will be very easy for them to find themselves being offered to try more drugs than they ever thought they would.

Moreover, even occasional users buy drugs from dealers, some of whom are people who kill to protect their interests, who use children to sell drugs, who encourage others to become drug addicts, all the while appearing to be nice guys. The point here is that using drugs has serious consequences for everyone: the people who use drugs socially once a month as well as those who are addicted.

Being honest with children has a simple benefit—it increases a parent's credibility. A parent who issues blanket statements about the evil of drugs forfeits all leverage in explaining to a child why drugs are bad. Anyone can say that drugs lead to jail and that drugs can kill. But people who can say they know about drugs and their dangers, and have made a decision not to use drugs, are people a child is more likely to listen to and trust.

*The third key is to be a friend to your child.* If you have an open line of communication with him, if he has heard your voice all along, he will be able to hear you in a crisis. And as a friend, you will know about your child's other friends and which of them is likely to bring temptation to your door.

Being a friend to your child means spending more time with him and paying attention to him long before drugs are an issue—when he's 3 and 4, as well as when he's 12 and 13. It means including him in your activities and participating in his. It means creating opportunities for the whole family to have fun together—instead of dividing everything into the world of the adult and the world of the child—and showing him that you know how to let go and have a good time. Young people who are having fun and whose parents have always taken an active interest in their lives are not apt to feel bored or neglected, which means they are less likely to need drugs as a kick.

Part of being a friend to your child is helping him to develop a social consciousness. Volunteering with your children to work for antidrug programs, or programs to combat poverty and homelessness (all of which take a strongly antidrug stance) will reinforce the message about drugs you give them at home, and help them feel they are making a real contribution to the world.

*The fourth and last key is to understand that drugs are not an isolated incident in any child's life.* Drugs come into a child's life as one force among many. Parents must be flexible enough to understand that rebellion and experimentation are probable. But a parent who has helped his child develop self-confidence, who has acted as a real friend, will know that his child can be trusted during his own days of rebellion—and that he will live to tell about them.

For more information about drug prevention, education, and treatment programs, see Appendix H in the back of this book.

## SEX EDUCATION

Today the average age of first intercourse in this country is 16. A third of sexually active teenagers used no protection the first time they had sex. By the time they are 19, more than three-quarters of all American teenagers are sexually active, and more than 1 million of them—one in ten, ages 15 to 19—get pregnant *each year*.

Whenever we contemplate such troubling statistics, its only natural to ask, can't sex education do better than this? After all, most kids (more than 60 percent) do get some sort of sex education today.

Certainly with all of the recent discussion over condom distribution in the schools, AIDS information, and family-life curricula, many of us have been left with the impression that kindergartners in the United States today are more familiar with in vitro fertilization and condoms than they are with their ABCs.

In fact, they are not. The sex education that most of our children are getting is shockingly modest. Some of the most widely taught sex education curricula actually include *less* information about such topics as abortion, contraception, and homosexuality than was offered in public schools a generation ago.

Unfortunately, a disturbingly large proportion of students are sexually active *before* their sex education courses begin. In a recent survey, most teachers said that sex education today is a matter of too little too late. Most children receive *no* sex education until the fifth grade.

The way that your school district decides how much your child should be taught, and when, is somewhat surprising. There are no federal guidelines on sex education. State guidelines vary widely, from New Jersey's liberal stance (comprehensive education in human sexuality is required in both elementary and secondary schools beginning with kindergarten) to Utah's conservatism (contraceptive information is off-limits). Most states, though, are far less specific, simply encouraging some sort of literacy in reproductive matters.

State mandates, however, are not as crucial as you might imagine. In fact, studies have failed to find a significant relationship between state and school district policies on sex education. And even your school district's policies may have little to do with what goes on in your child's classroom. "Sex ed is no different from reading," says Debra Haffner, executive director of the Sex Information and Education Council of the United States (SIECUS). "Whether your child's experience is fabulous or mediocre is going to depend on the teacher," says Haffner.

You should be aware that when your child enters kindergarten, there is a chance that he may be taught some form of sex ed ranging from simple concepts such as all living things reproduce to more specific facts like anatomical names and "good touches versus bad touches" (helping children to recognize if they are being sexually abused). Ask your school board or your child's teacher for a copy of the sex education curriculum in your school.

Asking if sex education works is almost a meaningless question. Many parents make demands of sex ed that they wouldn't make of any other subject. Schools can stress abstinence, but children learn values from their parents.

# Chapter 7

# WHAT ABOUT . . . TELEVISION? . . . COMPUTERS?

## TELEVISION

What would happen if your family television set was taken from your home for one week? Would you and your family be bored and frustrated with nothing to occupy your time? If so, you should examine your television viewing habits and consider some important facts concerning children and television.

A frightening amount of the research on children and television finds that time spent by preschoolers watching television is not only wasted, but undoubtedly harmful. To illustrate this point, Paul Copperman, author of *The Literary Hoax*, makes a valid point when he asks parents to consider what a child misses during those hours he spends in front of the TV screen. "He is not working in the garage with his father, or in the garden with his mother. He is not doing homework, or reading, or collecting stamps. He is not cleaning his room, washing the supper dishes, or cutting the lawn. He is not listening to a discussion about community politics among his parents and friends. He is not playing baseball or going fishing, or painting pictures. Exactly what does television offer that is so valuable that it can replace all these activities?"

Many parents today have the attitude, "What's the big deal? I watched television when I was growing up and I turned out alright. Besides, the shows she watches are cartoons, and those are made for kids." But the truth is television has changed dramatically from when the parents of today were growing up. Morals and values were sprinkled in every episode and violence was practically nonexistent. Sex was nowhere to be found and married couples slept in separate single beds!

As for cartoons being designed for children, studies show that some cartoons actually influence children to behave more aggressively, which is easy to understand when you stop to consider that the average cartoon has 25 or more violent acts per hour. Here are some facts about television to consider.

- Some researchers conclude that heavy TV viewers do not develop the more reflective style of thought necessary for learning in school settings.
- Many teachers report that students who are heavy viewers seem to be generally more passive and less energetic or motivated than those students who spend their free time reading, enjoying a hobby or sport, or simply playing outdoors.
- Television presents material in a manner opposite to that of a classroom, visually as opposed to verbally.
- The scenes on an average television show shift every 4 seconds. A child who is used to this sort of stimulation is sure to be bored in a classroom, and as a result, her eyes bounce around the room in an attempt to reestablish the level of stimulation she has grown use to.
- Studies show that in heavy viewers, television fosters a short attention span and inhibits the ability to listen and look carefully.
- Watching television trains one's eyes to stare rather than to scan. Scanning is an important skill needed in learning to read.
- Television interrupts the most important language lesson in the child's life, family conversation. If you are one of the millions of households in America that eats dinner in front of the TV set, please stop to consider what message this is sending to your child; that television is more important than conversation. The dinner hour is an ideal time for families to grow closer together and communicate with one another. Don't rob your family of this important time because of a sit-com.
- Television can desensitize the child's sense of sympathy for suffering and death.
- While television can stimulate a child's inner feelings, (raises doubts, fears, questions, emotions), it does not help her *deal* with these things. Only if parents watch shows with their children can these inner feelings and questions be dealt with effectively.
- If your child's play consists of increased rough and tumble activity at home or in preschool, she may be watching too much television that portrays fighting. Even some cartoon shows depict combat and aggression as sources of fun and entertainment. Some children will need adult guidance to avoid that kind of message.
- Television perpetuates stereotypes. Males outnumber females three to one on television; women tend to be portrayed in more deferential roles.

- A *Consumer Reports* statistic reports that "most children watch between 30,000 and 40,000 television commercials a year." Although adults might ignore television commercials, young children generally fail to distinguish them from other material presented.
- Watching frightening television scenes and scary movies can stimulate fears and night terrors in young children.
- Television can stifle the imagination by replacing the time a child would normally spend in free, exploratory, imaginative play.
- Watching television *requires* no learning, you just do it. Conversely, play involves exploration, activity, and fantasy and reading requires involvement and is an active problem-solving exercise.

Extensive research on the effects of television on children indicates that its potentially harmful *as well as* beneficial effects depend on many factors, an important one being the parent. How many hours a week does your child spend watching television? Sit down and honestly figure how many hours she has watched in the last 48 hours. Do you make sure you know what she watches? Are you happy about your child watching as much television as she does?

How much television is enough? The American Academy of Pediatrics recommends from one to two hours of *quality* programming per day is long enough for a preschooler. One way to think about this question is to ask yourself, what else could she be doing instead of watching television? If it is a time when you are busy and cannot supervise outdoor play or be directly involved in her activity for some reason, or the weather keeps you inside for extended periods, then perhaps carefully selected television viewing is a reasonable use of her time. If, however, your child could be engaged in creative play (alone or with others), outdoor activity, satisfying physical activity, or helping you with simple but important chores, then it would be appropriate to turn off the television. A child might protest and fuss when the set is first turned off. But if you stick with your decision about what is best, she will accept it eventually.

If you are unable to monitor your child's choice of television shows at any given time, you may want to consider calling your local cable company and requesting a certain channel to be "blocked" from your television set. There is no fee for this service and it allows you to act as a censor for your child's viewing, even when you are not present.

## Some Benefits of Television

On the positive side, television used appropriately and correctly, is one of the most valuable inventions of the twentieth century, and because of it, our children's understanding of the world around them is light-years ahead of pre-TV generations. Thanks to television, our children have a much greater knowledge of the four corners of the earth; they have seen and listened to major world leaders and experts in every field and have "attended" live historical events such as presidential inaugurations, congressional sessions, and space shuttle launches. Their imaginations have been stimulated, they have seen examples of prosocial behavior, learned letters and numerals, expanded concepts such as math and science, and increased prereading skills.

With television, a child living on a farm can see how people live in urban areas, and an only child can get a taste of what it is to live in a large family. When school age children learn about diversity, it helps them develop a deeper understanding of others and themselves.

Television viewing also serves as an important role as a stress reducer. Many bright, talented children routinely flop in front of the television after school and half watch, half sleep for a half hour or so before getting on with their music lesson, sports, practices, or homework.

A similar situation occurs with children who live in joint-custody situations, spending part of the week with one parent and part of the week with the other. Many begin their stay at the designated parent's home with an hour of television as they make the adjustments necessary to the change in environment.

What sort of television is worth watching for a preschool child? Programs geared to young children which make an effort to:

- present positive role models
- to solve problems by thinking and talking rather than by physical force
- teach concepts.

Shows such as *Mister Rogers' Neighborhood, Sesame Street, Barney and Friends, National Geographic Specials,* and science and nature shows usually carried by the Public Broadcasting System (PBS) station, are all wonderful examples of quality television for children. Animal shows, familiar stories, nonviolent fairy tales, and certain cartoons are also good.

Avoid programs that show animals or humans in great danger, that are especially scary, or that are far beyond a child's comprehension. News programs should probably be avoided given their penchant for gory and tragic stories.

Until you are reasonably confident that the programs your youngster is watching meet with your approval, it is a good idea to watch them with her. In this way you can catch messages that may need to be clarified or even contradicted. Use commercials and the time in between programs to help children cope with what they see by asking questions ("Why do you think that happened? What do you think will happen next?") and sometimes making clear value statements ("He shouldn't have done that!"). It can also be reassuring to encourage your child to look for all the helpers in a tragic or disaster situation.

Discuss the motives that underlay the character's actions to help children understand and clarify misconceptions. Help your child to distinguish between fantasy and reality: "Could this really happen?" Explain difficult words and ideas. Encourage your child's cognitive development by asking "What do you think will happen next? Why?" After the show, encourage recall by asking, "What color was the car Ernie drove?"

## Parents Make the Real Difference

Parents must take responsibility for their childrens' television viewing and set limits on it. Make the limits clear, "We can pick two short shows to watch together." Use a timer to signal when it is time to turn the TV off. Plan other activities. Make a commitment to fill the void. Give your child paper and crayons, go for a walk together, try out a new recipe in the kitchen, go to the library, or simply make yourself available for a talk. By providing appealing alternatives, you can help your child to voluntarily shake the TV habit.

Just as important as your child's television habits are your own. Modify your viewing habits if you use the TV as background noise while doing something else. Your children may be watching. Although you may be able to tune out negative messages and blatant distortions, young children cannot. They are coming away with impressions. You can't make them turn away from violence and watch only the happy moments. Much research indicates that if parents watch a lot of violence, their children do too. Furthermore, their children are more likely to act aggressively. Ask yourself whether you are a good model of a TV viewer to your children.

In the final analysis, television is like any other form of technology; its value depends on how it is used. While there is no plus in having children who are couch potatoes, wise and thoughtful parents can use television as a helpful child-rearing tool.

## WHAT ABOUT . . . COMPUTERS?

Computers are certainly a vital part of our modern world, and lack of computer knowledge will translate into a lack of job opportunities down the road, but does that mean that every parent of a preschooler should rush out and buy one? Certainly not. Computers can be an effective learning tool *if* they are used on a playful and limited basis, suited to a child's level of development. Computers can never replace first-hand experiences with real objects and events. Computers are most appropriate for children who are ready to make a transition from relying on actual objects and events to abstract thinking. In Piaget's terms, (discussed in Chapter 2) these are the children who are moving from preoperational to concrete operational thinking. Many children will begin this transition at the end of the preschool period. For others, it will come later. The important point is that computers will not help children "hurry" through the preschool period when direct, hands-on experiences are essential to development.

Most kindergarten and first grade school curriculums include some type of introduction to computers and for most children, this is the most appropriate time to expose them to the world of computers. Let's consider some points for and against computers.

### Arguments for Computers

Computers can challenge children to make connections and explore how things work. They are said to foster creativity, problem-solving skills, hand-eye coordination, and concentration. They also have developed longer attention spans, high levels of motivation, and a sense of control in some children who use them.

Anselmo and Zinck, two early childhood educators conducted research on children and computer use in 1987 and found that the computers promoted skill development in comprehension, memory, evaluation, problem solving, and creativity. Furthermore, cooperation was fostered as the children helped one another and worked together. The researchers concluded that if used in developmentally appropriate ways, computers could stimulate thinking skills.

Computers provide immediate feedback, helping a child know whether her approach to a problem is going to take her forward or lead to a dead end.

When a child makes a mistake on a drawing or a composition, instead of feeling discouraged or compelled to start over from scratch, she can cleanly erase it with a few clicks of the computer mouse, and then go back and try something new.

## Arguments Against Computers

There are a few arguments against computers in the early years. Many educational experts worry about rushing youngsters into the adult world of technology without fully understanding children's early development and the very serious limitations of the computer. They raise the following concerns.

Young children learn best by direct, hands-on experience; computers present abstractions. The computer is two-dimensional and the child cannot touch or physically manipulate the image on the screen. Concepts such as left, right, above, and below are best learned and understood when children move and orient their bodies and objects in space.

Computers limit experimentation and flexibility because the computer's responses are programmed and therefore restricted. But in the world of children's play, anything is possible and the child can determine the outcome.

Some implicit lessons of computers are not beneficial because they reinforce a particular style of learning akin to TV viewing. Instead children need to experience open-ended situations where there is no single right way to do things.

Many software programs are inappropriate for young children: they present drills, are violent, or require too much reading. "The majority of the software that's available was designed without a real understanding of children's developmental needs," says Susan Haugland, a professor of human environmental studies at Southeast Missouri State University, who has tested hundreds of programs with preschoolers. "They offer little more than rote learning tasks, not unlike the way flash cards are used for spelling and math drills," she says. "They ask for correct responses rather than developing smart thinking."

## Quality Software

There are a handful of software programs available that earn consistently high marks. Among those are *Kid Works* (Davidson & Associates), which allows youngsters to link words, pictures, and symbols to create "talking picture" stories; *Reader Rabbit's Ready for Letters* (The Learning Company), a collection of six activities that include finding ingredients to make a recipe in Grandma's kitchen and selecting pictures to match the sentences; *Millie's Math House* (Edmark), a creative arithmetic program in which Millie, a talking cow, invites kids to match shoes to feet according to size, decorate a bug, and count jellybeans used by a cookie machine; and *The Playroom* (Broderbund), a whimsical tour through a child's bedroom, where surprises and games that deal with learning to tell time or making silly animals out of different creatures' features wait behind various objects.

## Choosing Software

When choosing software for preschoolers, parents should keep a few important features in mind:

- Once the computer is turned on, the program should either begin automatically or after the child clicks the mouse on a visual symbol.
- The instructions should be conveyed through a computerized voice or graphics, rather than in writing, so young children can easily understand them.
- The program should be easy enough to use that adult supervision is unnecessary after the first session.
- The software should be interactive, meaning that the child is a participant rather than a spectator. By presenting children with numbers and letters to learn, shapes to pair, or objects and situations to change and explore, the program should draw children into the games and exercises.
- To ensure that youngsters don't get bored, the software should offer multiple levels of difficulty and a wide range of subject matter.

Initially, it should be easy to operate, expanding in complexity as a child masters skills and becomes ready to take on new challenges.
- Most of all, good educational software should be fun.

### What Parents Can Do

Here are some general guidelines to using a computer wisely:

1. Don't rely on the computer as a babysitter.
2. Participate when your child uses the computer. Make it part of the time you enjoy spending together.
3. As mentioned earlier, be very selective about software. Look for programs that are developmentally appropriate for preschoolers.
4. Let your children proceed at their own pace. Do not force time in front of the computer.
5. Encourage your children to play and have a variety of hands-on experiences as the basis for concepts and abstractions. With this as a foundation, your children will be better able to use the computer in a meaningful, creative way as they grow.

## WHAT ABOUT . . . VIDEO GAMES?

According to the American Optometric Association, video game playing, *in moderation,* may actually help sharpen vision skills.

Eye-movement skills, important for reading, may be sharpened. Eye-hand coordination, visual reaction time, and visual adjustability (the ability to make quick refinements and changes of movement utilizing eye-hand coordination) may also be improved by playing video games. These are skills necessary for driving a car, playing many sports, and performing some jobs.

Of course, the key phrase here is *in moderation.* Prolonged playing can strain the eyes, resulting in headaches; fatigue; blurred vision; itching burning eyes; and other symptoms. In children and teens, it may actually contribute to nearsightedness.

What is moderation? Strain occurs at different times for different people, so optometrists suggest instead that children play *no more than* 30 minutes without a break. During breaks children should go outside and look at things in the distance to give their eyes a rest from close visual tasks. And if children experience any of the symptoms of strain noted, they should discontinue playing video games.

As with television, and computers, *video games should not replace creative play or take up an unusual amount of a child's time.*

# Chapter 8

# GRADE "A" BOOKS, MUSIC, VIDEOS, TOYS

## BOOKS

The books listed in this section are arranged by subject matter and represent an appropriate selection for a child between 4 and 7 years of age. If you cannot find a particular title you are interested in, ask your librarian to order the book for you. Ideally a child will have been exposed to at least one book from each subject matter, with the exception of the books on AIDS, divorce, adoption, and death. These books are best left until the subject is raised by the child or a particular situation.

### Adoption

*Abby* by Jeannette Caines (Harper Collins)
*I Am Adopted* by Susan Lapsley (Bradbury Press)
*Is That Your Sister? A True Story of Adoption* by Catherine Bunin and Sherry Bunin (Pantheon)

### AIDS

*Children and the AIDS Virus* by Rosmarie Hausherr (Clarion Books) The immune system and AIDS is explained in simple clear language for elementary-age children. To order — 1-800-677-7760

### Alphabet Books

*The Accidental Zucchini* by Max Grover (Harcourt Brace)
*A Apple Pie* by Kate Greenaway (Warne)
*Alison's Zinnia* by Anita Lobel (Greenwillow)
*Alphabet Parade* by Seymour Chwast (Gulliver/Harcourt Brace and Jovanovich)
*C is for Curious: An ABC of Feelings* by Woodleigh Hubbard (Chronicle)
*City Seen from A to Z* by Rachel Isadora (Greenwillow)

***From Acorn to Zoo & Everything In Between in Alphabetical Order*** by
  Satoshi Kitamura (Farrar, Straus and Giroux)
***On Market Street*** by Arnold Lobel (Greenwillow)

## Animal Stories

***The Animal Kingdom*** by Jenny Wood (Macmillan)
***Curious George*** by H. A. Rey (Houghton Mifflin)
***Dinosaur Encore*** by Patricia Mullins (Harper Collins)
***Frog and Toad are Friends*** by Arnold Lobel (Harper)
***Have You Seen My Duckling?*** by Nancy Tafuri (Greenwillow)
***The Very Quiet Cricket*** by Eric Carle (Philomel)

## Classic Retellings

***Goldilocks and the Three Bears*** by Jonathan Langley (Harper Collins)
  (The '90s version)
***Mary Had A Little Lamb*** by Sarah Joseph Hale (Scholastic)
***The Three Billy Goats Gruff*** by Marcia Brown (Harcourt)
***The True Story of the Three Little Pigs*** by Jon Scieszka (Viking Kestrel)
  (told from the wolf's point of view)

## Colors

***Colors*** by Pascale de Bourgoing (Scholastic)
***Color Zoo*** by Lois Ehlert (J.B. Lippincott)
***John Burningham's Colors*** by John Burningham (Crown)
***Mouse Paint*** by Ellen Stoll Walsh (Harcourt Brace)
***Red Light, Green Light*** by Margaret Wise Brown (Scholastic)

## Coping With Anger

***The Hating Book*** by Charlotte Zolotow (Harper & Row)

## Counting or Math Concept Books

***1,2,3 to the Zoo*** by Eric Carle (Philomel)
***Count and See*** by Tanya Hoban (Macmillan)
***Counting Zoo*** by Lynette Ruschak (Aladdin)
***How Many?*** by Debbie MacKinnon (Dial)
***Is it Larger? Is it Smaller?*** by Tanya Hoban (Greenwillow)
***Millions of Cats*** by Wanda Ga'g (Coward McCann)
***The Noisy Counting Book*** by Susan Schade and Jon Buller (Random)

*One Hungry Monster, A Counting Book In .*
  O'Keefe (Little, Brown and Company)
*Shapes, Shapes, Shapes* by Tanya Hoban (Gre(
*Ten, Nine, Eight* by Molly Bang (Greenwillow
*When Sheep Cannot Sleep* by Satoshi Kitamura (
*Why Count Sheep?* by Karen Wallace (Hyperio

### Death

*The Dead Bird* by Margaret Wise Brown (Harpe
*My Grandpa Died Today* by Joan Fassler (Huma
*The Tenth Good Thing About Barney* by Judith '

### Dictionaries

*My First Dictionary* (Harper Collins) Includes 40(
  for 6–9-year-olds.
*Words for New Readers* (Harper Collins) 1,500 words. Good for 5–7-year-
  olds.

### Divorce

*Divorce is a Grown-Up Problem* by Janet Sinberg (Hazeldon)
*Emily and the Klunky Baby and the Next-door Dog* by Joan Lexau (Dial)
*Where is Daddy? The Story of A Divorce* by Beth Goff (Beacon Press)
*On Divorce: An Open Family Book for Parents And Children Together* by
  Sara Bonnett Stein (Walker & Co.)

### Doctor Visits

*Betsy and the Doctor* by Gunilla Wolde (Random House).
*Going to the Doctor* (A Mister Rogers' First Experience Book) by Fred
  Rogers (Putnam).
*Going to the Doctor: A Pop-Up Book* by Stacie Strong (Simon & Schuster).
*My Doctor* by Harlow Rockwell (Macmillan).
*When I See My Doctor* by Susan Kuklin (Bradbury).

### Encyclopedias

*The Doubleday Children's Encyclopedia* The perfect homework aid or
  curiosity companion, this handsome four-volume boxed set includes
  1,300 up-to-the-minute entries and more than 2,000 illustrations.
*New Book Of Knowledge* (Grolier) Written for elementary students, with
  large type and subjects that are of interest to children.

**Fantasy**

*Garth Pig Steals the Show* by Mary Rayner (Dutton)
*How I Captured a Dinosaur* by Henry Schwartz (Orchard)
*James in the House of Aunt Prudence* by Timothy Bush (Crown)
*Martha Speaks* by Susan Meddaugh (Houghton Mifflin)
*Where the Wild Things Are* by Maurice Sendak (Harper & Row)

**Folk and Fairy Tales**

*Iktomi and the Boulder* by Paul Goble (Orchard)
*Paul Bunyan* retold by Steven Kellogg (Mulberry/Morrow)
*Puss in Boots* by Charles Perrault (Farrar, Straus and Giroux)
*Sh-Ko and His Eight Wicked Brothers* retold by Ashley Bryan (Atheneum)
*The Story of Chicken Licken* by Jan Ormerod (Lothrop, Lee and Shepard)

**Going To Kindergarten**

*Annabelle Swift, Kindergartner* by Amy Schwartz (Orchard)
*Chrysanthemum* by Kevin Henkes (Greenwillow)
*Leo the Late Bloomer* by Robert Kraus (Windmill Books)
*Ramona the Pest* by Beverly Cleary (Morrow)
*Will I Have a Friend?* by Miriam Cohen (Macmillan)

**Handicaps**

*The Handmade Alphabet* by Laura Rankin (Dial) (teaches sign language)
*Howie Helps Himself* by Joan Fassler (Whitman)
*I Have a Sister, My Sister is Deaf* by Jean Whitehouse (Harper Collins)
*One Little Girl* by Joan Fassler (Human Science Press)

**Humorous Books**

*The Adventures of Isabel* by Ogden Nash (Joy Street/Little, Brown & Co.)
*Hey Willy, See the Pyramids* by Maria Kalman (Viking/Kestrel)
*If You Give a Moose a Muffin* by Laura Joffe Numeroff (Harper Collins)
*John Patrick Norman McHennessey—The Boy Who Was Always Late* by John Burningham (Crown)

**Land, Sea and Sky**

*Amos Camps Out: A Couch Adventure in the Woods* by Susan Seligson (Joy Street)

*The Carrot Seed* by Ruth Krauss (Harper)
*Down at the Bottom of the Deep Dark Sea* by Rebecca C. Jones (Bradbury)
*God's Paintbrush* by Sandy Eisenberg Sasso (Jewish Lights)
*Look What I Found* by Nick Sharratt (Candlewick) A lift-the-flaps book.
*Night of the Moonjellies* by Marka Shasha (Simon & Schuster)
*The Pig in the Pond* by Martin Waddell (Candlewick)
*Sailing To the Sea* by Mary-Claire Helldorfer (Viking)
*Starry Night* by David Spohn (Lothrop, Lee & Shepard)
*Zip, Whiz, Zoom!* by Stephanie Calmenson (Joy Street)

**Manners**

*No Bad Bears* by Michele D. Clise (Viking)
*Perfect Pigs* by Marc Brown and Stephen Krensky (Little, Brown & Co.)
*What Do You Say Dear?* by Sesyle Joslin (Harper Collins)

**Moms and Dads**

*Daddies* by Adele A. Greenspun (Philomel)
*Mama, Do You Love Me?* by Barbara Joosse (Chronicle)
*Trade-In Mother* by Marisabina Russo (Greenwillow)

**Miscellaneous**

*Alexander and the Terrible, Horrible, No Good, Very Bad Day* by Judith
    Viorst (Atheneum)
*Caps For Sale* by Esphyr Slobodkina (Harper Collins)
*The Little Engine That Could* by Watty Piper (Platt & Munk)
*Tasha Tudor's Five Senses* by Tasha Tudor (Platt & Munk)

**Multicultural Books**

*Anno's Britain* by Mitsumasa Anno (Philomel Books)
*Anno's Italy* by Mitsumasa Anno (Philomel Books)
*Family Pictures* by Carmen Lomas Garza (Children's Book Press)
*Looking For Daniela, A Romantic Adventure* by Steven Kroll and Anita
    Lobel (Holiday House)
*Mrs. Moskowitz and the Sabbath Candlesticks* by Amy Schwartz (Jewish
    Publications)
*Nadia the Willful* by Sue Alexander (Pantheon)
*The People Could Fly: American Black Folktales* by Virginia Hamilton
    (Knopf)

**New Baby**

**Arthur's Baby** by Marc Brown (Little, Brown & Co.)
**A Baby Sister For Frances** by Russell Hoban (Harper Collins)
**Julius, the Baby of the World** by Kevin Henkes (Greenwillow)
**Silly Baby** by Judith Casely (Greenwillow)

**Participation Books**

*Can You Guess?* by Margaret Miller (Greenwillow)
*The Great Waldo Search* by Martin Handford (Little, Brown & Co.)
   Great for visual discrimination.

**People and Places**

*An Auto Mechanic* by Douglas Florian (Greenwillow)
*Circus* by Lois Ehlert (Harper Collins)
*I Want To Be An Astronaut* by Byron Barton (Harper Collins)

**Resource Books (One Volume)**

*Animal Atlas* by Barbara Taylor (Knopf)
*Eyewitness Jr. Books* (Knopf) Very interesting, beautifully illustrated.
*Random House Children's Encyclopedia* (Random House) This book
   won't replace the multi-volume set of encyclopedias but it sparks
   children's interest in many different subjects.

**Rhyming Books**

*Each Peach Pear Plum* by Janet and Allen Ahlberg (Viking)
*Green Eggs and Ham* by Dr. Seuss (Random House)
*The Hungry Thing* by Jan Slepian and Ann Seidler (Scholastic)
*Sheep Out To Eat* by Nancy Shaw (Houghton Mifflin)

**School**

*Annie, Bea, and Chi Chi Dolores: A School Day Alphabet* by Donna
   Maurer (Orchard Books)
*Bus Riders* by Sharon Phillips Denslow (Four Winds Press)
*Maisy Goes To School* by Lucy Cousins (Candlewick Press)
*Masai And I* by Virginia Kroll (Four Winds Press)
*Mouse Views: What the Class Pet Saw* by Bruce McMillan (Holiday
   House)
*Red Day, Green Day* by Edith Kunhardt (Greenwillow Books)

*The School Mouse* by Dorothy Joan Harris (Frederick Warne & Co.)
(Great for school anxiety)

### Seasonal Stories

*My First Look At the Seasons* by Random House
*Snowsong Whistling* by Karen Lotz (Dutton)
*The Snowy Day* by Ezra Jack Keats (Viking)
*Weather: A First Discovery Book* by Gallimard Jeunesse and Pascale de
Bourgoing (Scholastic)

### Separation

*Be Good Harry* by Mary Chalmers (Harper & Row)
*Daddy and Ben Together* by Miriam Stecher and Alice Kandell (Lothrop,
Lee & Shepard)
*Don't Forget To Come Back* by Robie Harris (Knopf)
*Owen* by Kevin Henkes (Greenwillow)
*The Runaway Bunny* by Margaret Wise Brown (Harper Collins)
*Where's Our Mama?* by Diane Goode (Dutton)

### Sibling Relationships

*Big Sister Little Sister* by Charlotte Zolotow (Harper & Row)
*Do You Know What I'll Do?* by Charlotte Zolotow (Harper & Row)
*Dumb Stupid David* by Dorothy Aldis
*This Room Is Mine* by Betty Wright
*The Quarreling Book* by Charlotte Zolotov (Harper Collins)

### Sleepover

*Aunt Nina, Good Night* by Franz Brandenberg (Greenwillow)
*Ira Sleeps Over* by Bernard Waber (Houghton Mifflin)
*Staying At Sam's* by Jenny Hessell (Harper Collins)

### Starting Preschool

*Going To Daycare* by Fred Rogers (Mr. Rogers) (Putnam)
*Going To My Nursery School* by Susan Kuklin (Bradbury Press)

### Story Resources

*The Complete Fairy Tales and Stories* by Hans Christian Anderson
*Grimm's Tales for Young and Old* translated by Ralph Manheim
*Favorite Folktales From Around the World* by Jane Yolen

*The Storyvine: A Source Book of Unusual and Easy-to-Tell Stories From Around the World* by Anne Pellowski
*Grandfather Tales* by Richard Chase
*More Tales of Uncle Remus* retold by Julius Lester

**Teaching Positional Words**

*Over Under and Through* by Tanya Hoban (Macmillan)
*Rosie's Walk* by Pat Hutchins (Macmillan)

**Transportation**

*Diggers and Dump Trucks* by Angela Royston (Aladdin)
*Freight Train* by Donald Crews (Greenwillow)
*Harry at the Airport* by Derek Radford (Aladdin)
*Mike Mulligan and His Steam Shovel* by Virginia Lee Burton (Houghton Mifflin)
*Pigs Aplenty, Pigs Galore* by David McPhail (Dutton)
*Plane Song* by Diane Siebert (Harper Collins)
*Polar Express* by Chris Van Allsburg (Houghton Mifflin)
*Trucks* by Byron Barton (Harper Collins)

For a more complete listing of books for children, refer to *The New York Times Parent's Guide To The Best Books For Children* by Eden Ross Lipson (Time Books).

# MUSIC

Music needs to be part of a child's education because through it we learn about ourselves and our society. It enables us to express ourselves whether we are the player or the listener. Create a love of music early in your child's life. Here is a general list to get you started:

**Music for Movement and Sing-a-long**

*Bethie's Really Silly Songs About Animals* (Discovery) Funny and lots of fun for parents and kids, features "Ivana the Iguana".
*Big Big World* (Bill Harley, A & M) Upbeat and fun to move to. Songs deal with a variety of issues including divorce, cleaning your room and saving the planet.
*Camels, Cats, and Rainbows* (Paul Strausman, A Gentle Wind) Includes "You Are My Sunshine," "The Ants Go Marching," and "Peanut Butter."

*Car Songs* (Kimbo) Twenty-two sing-a-long favorites including "Wheels on the Bus," "B–I–N–G–O," and "John Jacob Jingleheimer Schmidt."

*A Child's Celebration of Song* (Music for Little People) A hit parade of children's songs sung by Peter, Paul and Mary, Judy Garland and Kenny Loggins and more.

*Dancin' Magic* (Joanie Bartels, Discovery) Includes "The Hokey Pokey," "The Peppermint Twist," and "Rockin' Robin."

*Deep in the Jungle* (Joe Scruggs, Shadow Play) Includes classics like "The Eensy Weensy Spider" and "Old MacDonald."

*Dinosaur Rock* (Michele Valeri and Michael Stein, Harper Audio) Dinosaurs are celebrated on this rock 'n' roll, swing, and bluegrass recording.

*A Duck in New York City* (Oak Street Music) In a series of very funny songs, a duck makes its way through the Big Apple with the aid of vocalist Heather Bishop.

*For Our Children* (Disney) Recorded to benefit the Pediatric AIDS Foundation, includes such superstars as Elton John, Bruce Springsteen, and Sting who sing their versions of classic kid tunes.

*Little Richard: Shake it All About* (Disney) 12 classics including "Twinkle, Twinkle Little Star," and "The Hokey Pokey."

*Put on Your Green Shoes* (Sony) Dedicated to healing the planet, this album includes an all star cast; Willie Nelson, Tom Chapin, Dr. John, and more.

*Sharon, Lois and Bram Great Big Hits* (A & M) 31 favorites including "Pop! Goes the Weasel," and "She'll Be Coming 'Round The Mountain."

*Singable Songs For the Very Young* (Raffi) Includes "Down by the Bay" and many other favorite Raffi tunes.

### Folk Tunes

*Mail Myself to You* (Rounder) John McCutcheon sings about the wonderfulness of animals and people.

*Pete Seeger's Family Concert* (Sony) 12 favorites including "Skip to My Lou," and "This Land is Our Land."

*Peter, Paul and Mommy, Too* (Warner) Includes "Puff the Magic Dragon," and "I Know an Old Lady Who Swallowed a Fly." This is a classic, recorded in concert.

### Multicultural Music

*African-American Folk Rhythms* (Ella Jenkins and the Goodwill Spiritual Choir, Smithsonian Folkways) A great introduction to African-American spirituals.

*Joining Hands With Other Lands* (Kimbo) A multicultural selection of songs that celebrate our diversity.

*Shake It To The One That You Love* (adapted by Cheryl Warren Mattox et al., JTG) A collection of 26 songs includes gospel, jazz, reggae, and rhythm and blues. Some songs like "Hambone" will be familiar, others will be a joyful discovery.

## Country

*Country For Kids* (Disney) Includes top country singers such as Mary Chapin Carpenter, Emmy Lou Harris, and Glen Campbell.

## From Hollywood and Broadway

*A Child's Celebration of Showtunes* (Music for Little People) Includes showtunes from *Fiddler on the Roof, The King and I, Oliver, Peter Pan,* and *The Sound of Music.*

*Bing Crosby's Greatest Hits* (MCA) Includes "Ac-cent-tchu-ate the Positive," "Too-Ra-Loo-Ra-Loo-Ral," and "You Are My Sunshine."

## Classical

*Bernstein Favorites* (Sony) A wonderful introduction to classical music.

*The Classical Kids Collection* (The Children's Group) An introduction to classical music that kids love.

Check the Appendix C in the back of this book for music catalogs you can order.

## VIDEOS

Unlike their favorite television show, children see their favorite video dozens of times. This fact makes it a vehicle for learning regardless of the content of the video, or your intentions for it. For this reason, you should purchase videos for your children in a very careful manner. If a certain video contains one negative phrase or thought, and your child is watching that video again and again, the negative phrase or thought is being subconsciously reinforced. The more your child is exposed to this negativeness, the more accepting of it he becomes. He, in a sense, becomes desensitized to it and therefore more accepting of the attitude it conveys.

For instance, consider for a moment the popular Walt Disney movies. Upon careful contemplation, one may wonder if they have an aversion to mothers. In the movie Aladdin, Princess Jasmine's mother is dead, and the character Aladdin has no mother. In the movie Beauty and the Beast, Belle has no mother. In The Little Mermaid, Ariel has no mother. Pinocchio has no mother. Snow White and Cinderella have wicked step-mothers and Peter Pan doesn't even know what a mother is. And everybody knows what happened to Bambi's mother!

Of course, these movies are wonderful entertainment for children, but parents should accept the challenge of considering the hidden messages videos send, as well as the stereotypes they may reinforce. Act responsibly and preview or briefly research a video before you purchase it for your child. There are many videos on the market that teach skills or values *while they entertain.* With such a large selection to choose from, one would be foolish to pass up the opportunity to use videos as a learning tool. Consider the following questions when choosing videos.

1. What is the appropriate age range?

2. Does the video contain anything that might frighten or disturb your child?

3. Does the video contain any violence or aggression and if so, how are they handled?

4. Does the video present gender, ethnic, or cultural stereotyping?

5. Does the video inspire children's imaginations, learning, and/or play?

6. Is this a tape to buy or rent? How often will your child be able to watch the video and still find it interesting?

7. Don't forget about the library for borrowing free educational and entertaining videos.

Here are some suggestions to get you started.

*Aunt Merriwether's Adventures in the Backyard* (The Nature Company, 30 minutes, ages 5–10) This fascinating video introduces children to the many surprises hiding in their own backyards using microphotography (extremely magnified images). Leading the tour are animated characters, Aunt Merriwether and her nephew.

*Count It Higher, Great Music Videos From Sesame Street* (Sesame Street Home Video, Random House, 30 minutes ages 3–6) In a MTV spoof, Count von Count is veejay for some unforgettable tunes. Children will learn, laugh, and enjoy.

*Don't Eat the Pictures: Sesame Street at the Metropolitan Museum of Art* (Random House, 60 minutes, ages 4–6) The Sesame Street gang accidentally gets locked in overnight at the Metropolitan Museum of Art in New York City. This video is a wonderful introduction to fine art and art history.

***The Ezra Jack Keats Library*** (Children's Circle, 41 minutes, ages 4–10) Six tales from the beloved author, including "Peter's Chair", about a boy's acceptance of his new baby sister. The stories transcend time, place, and race and deal with the issues of family bonds and self-awareness.

***Even More Preschool Power!*** (Concept, 30 minutes, ages 1–6) Fifth in an excellent series that uses see-and-do Montessori methods. The eclectic curriculum includes how to stand on your head, bake cheese biscuits, wash dishes, work with scissors, care for gerbils, and make a coin disappear.

***Kids for Safety*** (Monterey, 30 minutes, ages 4–10) Using a music video format, this video gets kids interested in the usually boring subject of safety. Three sections deal with bicycle, fire, and personal safety; each includes adults and children demonstrating techniques that the kids then explain, plus original tunes and a "Flash Quiz" review.

***Making and Playing Homemade Instruments*** (Homespun, 60 minutes, ages 5–12) Three young friends learn how to make and play instruments, including bottle-cap castanets and a bleach bottle banjo. The materials are cheap, the directions easy, and the music is fun.

***Mr. Rogers' Neighborhood, A Series of Four Tapes Including, Music and Feelings, Dinosaurs and Monsters, When Parents Are Away, and What About Love?*** (CBS Fox, 60 minutes, ages 3–6) The tapes in this series are designed to help children confront and move through a specific developmental challenge.

***My First . . . Video*** (Sony Wonder, 50 minutes, 6 in the series, ages 5–12) Sony offers six in this intelligent series for children, ranging from music to science. Each video has good instructions and a sense of fun.

***Paws, Claws, Feathers and Fins*** (KidVidz, 30 minutes, ages 4–12) An important message here is that not all pets are right for all kids. Several youngsters explain why they picked their companion dog, cat, hamster, fish, bird, or other creature—and describe their experiences with feeding, care, and training.

***Shamu & You, A Series That Includes, Exploring the World of Birds, Exploring the World of Fish, Exploring the World of Mammals, and Exploring the World of Reptiles.*** (Video Treasures, 30 minutes, ages 4–12) a lively mix of film, animation and song. One of the most appealing elements is the use of real kids, who describe what they know about the creatures they are seeing.

**Sing-Along Earth Songs** (Children's Television Workshop, 30 minutes, ages 2–5) Grover and friends go hiking and discuss simple things kids can do to protect the environment. Kermit, Big Bird, Oscar, Cookie Monster, Bert and Ernie sing the virtues of not littering, conserving water, preventing air pollution, etc. Full color lyric book included.

**Start-To-Read Series from Sesame Street** (Children's Television Workshop/ Praxis Media and Random House, 30 minutes, ages 3–8) Each of the four tapes in this series includes three stories narrated by Big Bird. The text of the story appears at the bottom of the screen so that your child can "read along" with Big Bird.

**Thomas the Tank Engine and Friends** (Strand Home Video, 40 minutes, 12 in the series, ages 3–8) Thomas is the locomotive star of the popular PBS TV show **Shining Time Station.** Each tape in the series includes seven short stories that are designed to enhance children's social and emotional development.

**The Wee Sing Train** (Price Stern Sloan, 60 minutes, ages 2–8) Two children create a fantasy world in their playworld and are plunged right into it. While riding aboard a train, they join in singing such songs as "Home on the Range" and "I've Been Working on the Railroad" (lyric sheet is included). Eighth in the "Wee Sing . . . " series which is always filled with fantasy, antics and lots of singable tunes. Any of the videos in this series would be a good choice for a child who enjoys singing and music.

**Who's Afraid of Opera?** (Kultur, 60 minutes, ages 5–10) Joan Sutherland and friends keep a running commentary going on the sidelines of an abbreviated famous opera. There are four 60 minute videos in the series. The pace is fast; the style, overly dramatic—it's great exposure if you don't want your kids to think of opera as boring.

**Zoopolis** (David Lee Miller Productions, 60 minutes, ages 3–6) A tour of the Milwaukee County Zoo is hosted by Gilda Gorgeous, a real giraffe. This behind the scenes tour includes conversations with zookeepers and walks through the natural habitat where the animals live.

Check the Appendix C in the back of this book for a listing of video catalogs you can order.

## TOYS

Toys are much more important than many parents realize, because at the preschool age, *informal play is still the best path to learning.* Building a tower with blocks, they discover some very basic math concepts. Digging in the sand or floating leaves in puddles, they make early science discoveries. Good toys can ignite imagination, stimulate creativity, elicit striving, and provoke the desire to make order. They whet and saturate appetites. They help shape lifelong interests, lead to careers, focus passions. They push, pull, and comfort. They help a child build a sense of self, a sense of ability to accomplish.

Toys offer children a first chance at providing *themselves* with a body of knowledge. Many children will root their imaginative life and internalize physical laws in that knowledge.

Good toys are *not* instant gratification. They are not fast highs and quick crashes—they have staying power; they engage. They help build attention spans, not fragment them.

Good toys do not excite interminable materialism. They do not glamorize or reflect the destructive aspects of society. A good toy does not offer answers; it stimulates questions and presents problems for solving—all in good humor. Sometimes with wit.

When you buy toys for your child, choose carefully. Choose a toy that is just right for your child's stage of growing. Some toys will be too hard to use. A fifty-piece puzzle for a two year old is not appropriate. It would be much too frustrating for him and the pieces would end up being thrown around. A six piece puzzle would be much more appropriate.

Watch carefully *where* your child is on the learning ladder. Try to match the games and toys you provide with what your child is *ready* to learn.

Preschoolers are amazing learners. Watch and listen to your child at play and you can hear their busy minds working. Pretend play is their favorite. This gives them a chance to become big and powerful people. Providing props for such play gives children the learning tools to develop language, imagination and a better understanding of themselves and others.

Unlike the toddler who moved from one thing to another, preschoolers become able to really focus their attention on building a bridge of blocks, working on a puzzle or painting pictures. They enjoy solo play often.

What is your role in play? A child who has shelves full of stuffed animals or every piece of the hottest licensed character may seem to have tons of toys, but the truth is that, no matter how many *Turtles* or *Trolls* a kid has, such collections offer just one kind of play. Every now and then, take an inventory of your child's toy clutter to see what's really being played with and what needs to be packed away or donated.

Some parents have also found it helpful to rotate their child's toy collection. Pack away the things that aren't played with at the moment. After being hidden away in the closet for a few months, they will once again become favorites.

Here you will find a basic checklist of toys for preschoolers, followed by suggestions for each item on the list:

### Basic Check-list for Preschoolers

- Set of blocks
- Set of props (small vehicles, animals, people)
- Wheel toys—trikes and other vehicles
- Dolls and or soft animals and puppets
- Dress up clothes
- Housekeeping toys
- Transportation toys
- Art materials (crayons, paints, clay, etc.)
- Simple puzzles (8 pieces and up)
- Matching games
- Picture books
- Tape player and music and story tapes
- Sand and water toys
- Science toys
- Outside and active play toys

### Blocks

If there is one toy no child should be without, blocks are it. Stacking a tower, balancing a bridge, setting up a zoo, all call for imagination, dexterity, decision making, and problem solving. Built into the play are early math and language concepts that give concrete meaning to abstract words like "higher," "lower," "same," and "different." Best of all, blocks are wonderfully versatile—they build a space city today and a farm tomorrow. Children who enjoy characters like "Turtles" or "Mermaids" can even come up with their own settings. They will enjoy both wood and plastic types of blocks; each provides different kinds of valuable play experiences. Choosing blocks depends largely on your budget and space. Although many of these are expensive, they are a solid investment that your grandchildren may enjoy one day.

### Wooden Blocks

*Junior Unit Blocks* (T.C. Timbers $62.50) Smaller scaled set includes 140 pieces in 12 shapes including arches, columns, triangles, ramps, and buttresses. (800) 359-1233

*Unit Blocks* (Childcraft $109.95) Comes with 86 blocks in 12 shapes. (800) 631-5657

### Cardboard Blocks

*Giant Construction Blocks* (Constructive Playthings $15.95) Set of 12 printed like red bricks. Size— 12″ × 6″ × 4″. (800) 832-0572

### Plastic Blocks

If you decide to buy plastic blocks, you should keep in mind that they require a different kind of dexterity than do wooden or cardboard blocks. Beginners are better off with large pieces that make bigger and quicker constructions. For longest use, your best buy is probably to pick one system, high priced or otherwise, and build on it.

*Duplo Basic Bucket* (Lego $29) Includes a wheel base, and a bunny, pup, cat, and people faces for pretend play and building. (203) 763-4011

*Duplo Airport* (Lego $36) Includes control tower, helicopter, airplane, car, gas pump and play figures. (203) 763-4011

*Mega Blocks* (Ritvik $10 and up) A basic set comes with oversized plastic pegged blocks, wheels and angled pieces for vehicle construction. (800) 465-MEGA

### Props for Blocks

*Highway Rescue Fleet* (Heros/Darda $27) Six wooden vehicles include a fire truck, ambulance, police van, tractor trailer and tow truck with car in tow. (800) 638-1470

*Giant Flexible Dinosaur Collection* (Toys to Grow On $29.50) Eight dinosaurs made of colorful plastic. Assorted sizes with the stegosaurus measuring 16″ long. (800) 542-8338

*Wild Animal Set* (Constructive Playthings $19.95) Set of five wild animals includes a 12″ tall giraffe, an elephant, zebra, lion, and polar bear. Same company also makes Seven Farm Animal set. (800) 832-0572 *Noah's Ark* (T.C. Timbers $62.50) 32 painted wooden animals and Noah's family come aboard a handsome ark. (800) 359-6144

## Wheel Toys—Trikes and Other Vehicles

Many children still enjoy the vehicles with no pedals at this age, but now they are ready for tricycles and kiddie-cars with pedals. The battery-operated vehicles that go 5 mph look tempting, but they do nothing for your child's big muscle development. Here is what to look for in a three-wheel drive with pedal action:

- Bigger is not better, don't look for a trike to grow into.
- Take your child to the store to test drive the right size. Getting on and off should be safe with no need of adult assistance.
- Preschoolers need the security of a three wheeler that is more stable. Like *Kettrike Maxi* (Kettler $79 & up) (804) 427-2400 or for a long-legged preschooler, try the *Sports Cycle* (Little Tikes $45) which is scaled bigger than most. (800) 321-0183
- A primary color bike can be reused by younger siblings regardless of their sex.

**Hints for Bicycles:**

- Five year olds are ready for a bicycle with training wheels. Again, take your child to the store with you to make sure the size of the bike is right for your child. Buy one that fits instead of "one to grow into."
- When children straddle a bike, they should be able to put a foot on the ground for balance.
- Budget and size will dictate the choices of bikes.

*Hedstrom* ($100 & up), *Schwinn* ($130 & up), and *Huffy* ($100 & up) offer solidly built 16″ bikes with adjustable training wheels and an assortment of accessories.

- Wear a helmet! According to the Consumer Product Safety Commission, one in seven children suffers head injuries in bike-related accidents. While studies show that wearing helmets reduces the risk of injury by 85 percent, the sad fact is that only 5 percent of the bike riding kids actually wear helmets.

## Dolls, Hugables, and Puppets

*Bathbaby Girl or Boy* (Corolle/Brio $70) Gender specific dolls that reflect children's anatomies. Designed for tub use. Great for new big brothers or sisters who want to take care of a baby. (800) 558-6863

*Cabbage Patch Kids* (Hasbro $15 & up) Comes with easy on/off clothes, in girls or boys, African-American and Caucasian. (800) 752-9755

*Talking Barney* (Playskool $34.99) Says hundreds of Barney expressions. (800) 752-9755

- If your child already has several dolls he or she enjoys, consider buying strollers and furniture to go with the dolls, instead of buying new ones with no play accessories.

### Puppets and Puppet Stages

Through the mouths of puppets, kids can say or express feelings they might otherwise be too shy to reveal. So puppets are a unique outlet for venting feelings and developing imagination and language skills.

*Bug Puppets* (Folkmanis $12 & up) Hand puppets that fit like a glove. Choose from ladybugs, butterflies and insects. More expensive ones include friendly dogs and a bald eagle, among others. (510) 658-7677

*Pick A Puppet* (Creative Education of Canada $14) This is a versatile puppet set with two hand puppet bodies and velcro features that can be used to create many players. (800) 982-2642

*Sesame Street Puppets* (Applause $15 & up each) Puppets come in hand and full-body sizes. (800) 777-6990

*Puppet Stage* (Creative Education of Canada $12) Table top stage made of brightly colored corrugated recycled plastic is lightweight and folds for easy storage. (800) 982-2642

*Puppet Stage* (Childcraft $125) Top of the line wooden stage with curtain and shelves in back for storage. Can be reversed and used as a play store.

- If you don't want to spend the money, try using a large appliance box with a hole cut in it.

## Dress Up Play and Let's Pretend Props

Old and glittery clothes from the backs of closets or thriftshops are the basics, then you can add . . .

*Action Hats* (Childcraft $9.95) Set of six hats include firefighter, construction worker, racer, police cyclist with goggles and engineer. (800) 631-5657

*Doctor's Bag* (Fisher Price $15) Includes a pressure gauge, stethoscope, thermometer, bandage, and other necessities.

*Paraphernalia for Pretending* and the *Let's Pretend* kits from Creativity for Kids are good also. (216) 589-4800

## Housekeeping Tools

*Party Kitchen* (Little Tikes $80) Includes a combo stove, oven, sink, built-in coffeemaker, cordless phone, and drop side table for small people.

*The Compact Kitchen* (Little Tikes $60) Has sink, stove top, oven and microwave oven.

*Magic Vac* (Fisher Price $18) Pretend cleaner that lights up and makes popping sounds when pushed, needs no batteries.

*Press "N" Play Ironing Set* (Little Tikes $20) Designed for safe play.

*The Tea Set* (Battat $14.50) Four simple cups and saucers with serving tray, sugar and creamer.

*Cooking and Baking Set* (Battat $12.95) 13 piece set.

*Cordless Play Phone* (Little Tikes $10) Buttons to push, an antenna, a base with a directory dial to spin and no cord.

## Transportation Toys

*Big Dump Truck* (Little Tikes $23) (800) 321-0183

*Mighty Tonka Dump Truck* (Tonka $17) The classic metal model. (800) 752-9755

*Mighty Tractor Trailer With Bulldozer* (Tonka $50)

*Water Cannon Fire Truck* (Tonka $27)

*Cement Mixer* (Tonka $25)

*The Sound Machine Truck* (Nylint $39.95) Shiny black 18-wheeler. Turn key on back of rig and the engine starts. Has air-brake sounds when stopped and warning beeps when backing up. (800) 397-8697

*Parking Garage* (Back to Basics $99) A three-level wooden garage made for Matchbox-sized vehicles. Includes a service station, gas pumps, and service elevator to take cars to each level. (800) 356-5360

*Power & Sounds Garage* (Fisher Price $29.99) Includes a garage and a car wash. A mechanical "power drill" lets kids change tires and even the chassis of the car. (800) 432-5437

## Remote Control Vehicles

*Air Nikko* (Nikko $38) With real jet sounds and flashing lights. Sound can be turned on and off. (214) 422-0838

*Preschool Remote Control Car* (Playskool $30) Car spins and goes forward with the push of a button. (800) 752-9755

## First Trains and Track Toys

A nonelectric train is a classic toy that will keep growing in complexity as you add bridges, roundhouses and other features. Although many train owners glue their tracks down on a table top, much of the play value and potential for creativity is lost when you do this with young children. Young engineers enjoy changing their train route often and actually are learning when they do this. When buying a train set, buy enough track to make it interesting. The starter set with just a circle of track gets boring quickly. Its best to stick with one company since some of the brands are not compatible. Preschoolers are not ready for electric trains yet.

*Suspension Bridge Train Set* (Brio $69.95) Elaborate top of the line train set with 20 pieces of track, one suspension bridge with ascending tracks and supports, and a three piece magnetic train. This company also makes a circus train set. (800) 558-6863

*Wooden Train* (T.C. Timber $63.50) Comes with enough track to form a figure eight, a pass-through tunnel bridge and a train that fastens with magnets. Many accessories are available and these are compatible with the Brio set. (800) 359-1233

*Thomas The Tank Engine* (Learning Curve $69) Modeled after the Thomas Train on the PBS show, this set includes a 22-piece starter set with Thomas, track, and engine shed, RR sign, trees and play figures. Other trains are sold separately. Set is Brio compatible. (800) 776-6909

*Duplo Train and Track Set* (Lego $44) Pulled by a stout engine, the train cars carry cargo and passengers and combine nicely with Duplo blocks. (203) 763-4011

## Art Materials

Markers, crayons, chalk, clay or paint each provides different experiences, all of which invite children to express ideas and feelings, explore colors and shapes, and develop muscles and control needed for writing. A supply of basics should include:

- Big crayons
- Washable markers
- Glue Stick
- Tempera Paint
- Finger Paint
- Molding material such as Play-Doh (see the recipe for homemade play-dough in Chapter 5)
- Colored construction paper
- Plain paper
- Safety scissors

## Paints and Brushes

Tempera paint is ideal for young children because of its thick, opaque quality. Watercolors are more appropriate for school-age children. Young children will have more success with thick brushes rather than skinny ones, which are harder to control. To reduce the number of spills, invest in paint containers sold with lids and openings just wide enough for a thick paint brush. Buying paint in pint-sized squeeze bottles will be more economical than buying small jars of paint that will dry out. Look for both nontoxic and washable labels on all the art supplies you buy. (See Chapter 5 for a homemade fingerpaints recipe.)

*Sponge Painters* (Alex $3) Set of three foam painting tools. (201) 569-5757

*Finger Paints* (Crayola $1.49) A neat package of fingerpaints in three squeeze tubes. Use them outside and then use the hose to clean up the mess. (800) CRAYOLA

*Two-Sided Magna Doodle* (Tyco $20) Draw on either side, one is black and the other is white. The "eraser" is tied on so it won't get lost. (800) 367-8926

*Double Easel* (Little Tikes $60) A chalkboard on one side and a large clip that holds a pad of 17″ × 20″ paper on the other side. Has removable paint trays. (800) 321-0183

*My Paper Craft Case* (Alex $25) Carrying case comes with a large assortment of different kinds of paper, glue tube, glitter pen, scissors and an activity pamphlet for making fans, hats, finger puppets and flowers. Other kinds of kits available. (201) 569-5757

### Early Games and Puzzles

Preschoolers are not ready for complex games with lots of rules or those that require strategy skills. Your best bet for family fun are games of chance where players depend upon the luck of the draw rather than skill. The idea of taking turns as well as the concept of winning or losing is often hard to understand at this age. The games listed here can be played cooperatively or they are quick and short so that there can be lots of winners. Some of these games can even be played alone.

*Busy Gears* (Playskool $16 & up) There's no right or wrong way to arrange the variety of large and small gears and cranks on the pegboard base. This game is bright and interesting and teaches problem solving as well as cause and effect. It looks like a three-dimensional moving puzzle. (800) 752-9755

*Candyland* (Milton Bradley $6) The same one you knew as a child is a classic game for learning colors, counting, and taking turns. No reading required. (413) 525-6411

*Floor Dominoes* (Galt $14) Set of 28 double-sided dominoes with pictures to match on one side and bold color-coded dots on the other. Ideal for counting, picture and color matching. (800) 899-GALT

*Lottino* (Ravensburger $14.95) A matching game with colorful graphics that develops language as well as matching skills. (201) 831-1400

*Match-A–Balloon* (Ravensburger $14.95) Throw the colorful die and match the bright balloon on the playing board with the color thrown. First to cover all the balloons wins. An easy way to learn matching and colors. (201) 831-1400

*Mothers & Babies Match-Up* (Ravensburger $14) Instead of competing to win, here's a game that can be used for several cooperative or solo games. There are 18 pairs of animal mothers and babies that fit together in self-correcting, no-reading, matching games for children. (201) 831-1400

*Shape 'N' Color* (Anatex $18) A color-coded sorting board has five bright vinyl posts on which to sort 50 plastic chips by shape or color. Pattern cards are also included for another kind of challenge for eyes and hands. Comes in a plastic drawstring bag. (Be careful of small parts, and the drawstring bag may be dangerous.) (800) 999-9599

***Tools Puzzle*** (Lauri $10.95) Eight tools include saw, hammers, wrenches, screwdriver, and drill. They fit into the crepe foam rubber square puzzle frame. (207) 639-2000

### Lacing Games

***Jumbo Stringing Beads*** (T.C. Timbers $16.95) Stringing 27 large wooden beads in different colors and shapes is fun and will develop the refined hand movements needed for writing. (800) 359-1233

***Cotton Reels*** (Galt $9) These colorful plastic spools are good for sorting by color or stringing in patterns. (800) 899-4258

***Lacing Shapes*** (Lauri $6) Children love lacing the thread in and out of the holes in these rubbery animal shapes. (207) 639-2000

## Music

***Six-Piece Rhythm Band Set*** (Music for Little People $29.50) This set has a wonderful sound quality and includes six pieces; 5″ cymbals, jingle tap, hand castanet, 6″ tambourine, 5″ triangle and block. Ideal for dance and play-along games that develop physical movement, nonverbal expression and joy of music. (800) 346-4445

***Music Maestro II*** (Aristoplay $25) This game introduces the many sounds, shapes, and functions of 48 different instruments. It includes a game board and two cassette tapes of instrument sounds. Five games of graduated difficulty. Ages 4 and up. (800) 634-7738

## Sand and Water Toys

Sand and water are basic materials for exploring liquids and solids, floating and sinking, sifting and pouring. An inexpensive pail and shovel are basic gear and less upsetting to lose than the high priced spread. Tower molds are inexpensive and great fun for building castles.

***Aqua Play Canal System*** (Galt $60 & up) A system of interlocking blue plastic water ways provides a hands-on way to investigate how boats, locks, pumps, and waterwheels work. Expensive but unique. Can be used in an empty tub with swim suits on days too cold for outdoors. (800) 899-4258

***Deluxe Sand & Water Set*** (Battat $19.95) The ultimate ten-piece beach set: super size bucket with hose sprinkler, sandmill, small pail, molds, and other tools that fit under the sieve lid. (800) 274-8440

***Sand and Water Table*** (Playskool $60) This plastic table looks like a picnic table but comes with side-by-side wells for sand and water and a cover that converts the table for art projects or picnics. Can be used indoors or out. (800) 752-9755

## Science Toys

Floating a leaf in a puddle, collecting pebbles in the park, making mud pies in the sandbox, watching worms wiggle—these are a few of the active ways children learn about the natural world. Here are some favorites for early science exploration:

### Magnets and Observation Tools

***Magnetic Blocks*** (Battat $12.95) A playful introduction to the power of magnetism. Magnets are safely embedded in 16 brightly colored blocks. Can be built into moving vehicles with wheels. (518) 562-2200

***Giant Super Magnet*** (Marvel $3.95) A 13″ horseshoe magnet. Easy to hold and powerful enough to pick up several metal objects. (800) 832-0572

### Hardwood Giant Magnifiers

***Wooden-handled Magnifier*** (T.C. Timber $20) Pricey but beautifully crafted with an extra-big plastic safety lens for close-up looking. (800) 832-0572

***Magnifier*** (Marvel $19.95) The 11″ high, wooden stand holds the large, easy to use plastic magnifier, which provides a focused, blown-up view of what ever is placed below it. (800) 832-0572

### Garden Work

***Bubble Blower*** (Fisher Price $19) Turn the big blue crank to blow bubbles and real leaves. (800) 432-5437

***Garden Tools*** (Little Tikes $12) Plastic. (800) 321-0183

***Mulcher Mower*** (Little Tikes $25) Fake grass clippings fly in the see-through chute. Includes a turn key, a gas cap that opens to "fill 'er up" and good sound effects. (800) 321-0183

***Red Wagon*** (Radio Flyer $45) The classic vehicle for hauling. (800) 621-7613

*Garden Tractor and Cart* (Little Tikes $68) A pedal driven bright green tractor pulls a cart that detaches to become a wheelbarrow. Great for hauling tools and dirt. (800) 321-0183

## Active Physical Play

Active play builds muscles, coordination, and confidence in preschooler as able doers. It also establishes healthy active patterns for fitness, relieves stress, and provides a legitimate reason to run and shout. Agreeing on the rules of the game and taking turns promotes important social and cooperative skills. Swing sets and other large yard equipment are enjoyed at this time as are the toys listed.

*Boingo Ball* (Oddzon $18) A silky fabric cover wraps around this partially air-filled foam ball. Lightweight and big. (408) 866-2966

*Hydrant* (Fisher Price $19.99) Just attach to your lawn hose and water sprays out the side or top. (800) 432-5437

*Lady Bug Jumping Ball* (Togu/T.C. Timbers) A big 17" inflatable lady bug ball with two built-on handles to hold as child sits on top and bounces along. (800) 359-6144

*Octopus* (Little Tikes $80) Similar to a mini merry-go-round, this turquoise, plastic octopus-shaped toy can be used by several children for sitting or spinning. (216) 650-3000

### Stand-Alone Climbers

*Activity Gym* (Little Tikes $190) A durable climber with four colorful panels that lock together to form an all purpose play environment. Can be used indoors or out. (800) 321-0183

*Climbasaurus* (Flexible Flyer $80) Low to the ground climber, slide and hideaway cave in the shape of a bright blue and yellow dinosaur. Can be used indoors or out. (800) 521-6233

### Playhouses

*Country Cottage* (Little Tikes $200) Sturdy, pastel colored plastic. 52" high. (800) 321-0183

*Log Cabin* (Little Tikes $260) Larger, sturdy brown plastic. 6 feet high. (800) 321-0183

*Castle* (Little Tikes $275) Sturdy plastic with hidden escape passages, turrets and towers. (800) 321-0183

- Also consider the large appliance boxes cut and painted to look like a house. You and your child can have fun decorating it.

See Appendix C in the back of this book for a list of toy catalogs you can order.

# SECTION III
# AT SCHOOL

*Upon the education of the people of this country, the fate of this country depends.*

Benjamin Disraeli

# Chapter 9

# WHAT TO LOOK FOR IN A SCHOOL

Finding the right school for your child requires that you examine some key points about the programs you are considering and then make some visits to investigate. If you don't take the time to do this, your child could end up in a school filled with crowded classes, a poor curriculum, a bare bones budget, lack of parental involvement, and discipline and drug problems. This is certainly not an appropriate learning environment for any child. If you are planning on public schooling, it is necessary that you look at the offerings for the entire district because today, due to school closings, redrawing of attendance zones, and desegregation, living in a specific neighborhood does not always ensure attendance at a particular school. Finding a good private or parochial school demands the same criteria and diligence, not only to decide if the school is worth the money, but more importantly, if your child's particular needs will be met. Regardless of which type of school you choose for your child, the criteria are basically the same.

Here are some factors to consider:

## Building and Facilities

Although there are many wonderful schools operating out of less than desirable facilities, many times the simple physical attributes of a school will tell you a lot if you know what to look for. Look around at the general overall condition of the school. Is it adequate for the demands placed on it? Are the grounds well kept? A school that is not kept clean and in good repair says much about the institution's commitment to excellence. Here are a few features every good school should have:

1. A real library, not just a room full of books. Look for real research material, encyclopedias, journals, an extensive collection of magazines, newspapers, records, and video tapes. If there is not a computer in each classroom, look for one in the library. Take a few minutes to talk to the librarian. Ask her a few questions like, "Do you have a story time or

teach any lessons on specific topics?" "In what capacity do you work with the teachers?" Many librarians help the teachers supplement their teaching units by locating relevant materials for them. The atmosphere of the library should be geared toward the children and reading.

2. Is there a gymnasium? Check it out for safety and adequacy. Find out if the school has any organized sports teams.

3. What science materials are available? Are they current and plentiful enough for each child to experience them?

4. What do the individual classrooms look like? Are the walls covered with learning and visual aids as well as the children's art and school work? Are there plenty of books and helpful teaching materials within easy reach of the children? (See *Guidelines for Visiting Classrooms.*)

5. Be sure to check the restrooms and cafeteria. They should be clean and orderly. After all, your child will be using them every day.

6. Ask the principal if the school or school system has a philosophy of education. If so, request a copy for your own evaluation. Ask about the discipline policy. If you don't agree with it, talk with the principal to find out your options.

### Atmosphere

There cannot be good teaching and learning going on in a school that is not orderly. Walk the halls, sit in on a class or two, talk to the teachers, staff, and even the students. The atmosphere should be cooperative, not competitive and you should get the feeling that learning is fun and not forced. Look for examples of students' work displayed in the halls and classrooms. Are students praised and encouraged in a variety of ways? If you had to describe the feel of the school in just one word, what would that word be?

You will be shown much more attention if you call and make an appointment to visit the school first. Get a feel for the overall environment and make sure that it is a place that would be suitable for your child.

### Guidelines for Visiting Classrooms

Your first clue to the classroom is the choice the principal makes when he selects the one you may visit. You can tell a lot about his educational philosophy based on this. For example, if a principal takes you only into traditional classrooms, with desks in rows facing forward and only *A* papers on display, you might conclude that he believes in that educational approach. (Which is not necessarily the best.) The teacher and class he chooses will most likely be one of the ones *he* considers best. If he allows you to roam freely and visit any room you like, this is a good sign, indicating that he feels confident about his entire staff.

### Children's Reactions and Feelings

Be sure to spend a good part of your time in the classroom watching the children, instead of the teacher. Their faces, actions, and words will tell you whether or not they feel competent, valued, challenged, and motivated. Their interactions with one another and with the teacher will tell you a lot about what it's like to be a member of the class.

### The Classroom Setup

The way the classroom looks and how it is arranged can tell you a lot about how instruction is carried out and how children and teacher interact. The room should be cheerful and appealing with furniture and displays as well as important information at the right level for children.

Are there areas around the room where children can work independently? These are called *learning centers,* and usually accommodate two or three children. Each one is for a specific activity, such as experimenting with different writing tools and papers, or listening to a story played on a tape player. Also look for a quiet place in the room where a child can be alone and look at a book. A classroom organized this way allows for differing styles and paces of learning and enables children to pursue their own interests.

Look at the bulletin boards. Is work displayed from *all* of the students? Or just a handful of perfect ones? Do you see several duplicated pages or workbook assignments? Or is there evidence of more creativity tailored to this particular class?

Do you see signs around the room saying "Don't do this" or are the rules stated positively? "In the halls, we *walk quietly.*"

Is the room so neat it makes you wonder if things are on display but not used? Or is it so messy that it is unorganized and things are not taken care of and used properly? Look for a comfortable amount of "mess," or work in progress, and mostly clean, organized work areas where children can find what they need.

### The Classroom Atmosphere

How does it feel to be in the classroom? Is this a place you would want to spend six hours a day, five days a week? While the physical appearance of the room contributes to this feeling, the teacher's actions are even more important in helping create the atmosphere in many ways. How does she interact with the children? What message does she give with her face and tone of voice (not just her words)? Does she treat the children with love and respect? How does she get the children's attention? When they are noisy, does she yell and scream? Or does she have a trick to get them quiet, such as briefly turning off the lights, or holding up her hand? This shows you that she has control and that she assumes that there will be noise from time to time.

### Instructional Strategies

Here are a few things you can observe fairly quickly to get an idea of the instructional emphasis: Is there evidence of routines in the classroom? Can you see student projects either on display or in process? Is the instruction all teacher-directed, or are the children allowed to discover some things on their own or in small groups?

## Curriculum

This is one of the most important factors to consider when choosing a school for your child. Literacy and language development should form the core of any elementary school curriculum. Writing, speaking and listening skills should be taught alongside reading. The teacher's main goal should be to instill a love of reading and writing. The teacher should read to her class every day and expose and acquaint them with a rich variety of stories, rhymes, and plays. The next important subject is math, which should be taught through manipulatives in addition to the standard worksheet or workbook approach. Science and social studies are often not covered in depth at this point because the children have not yet mastered reading skills, but a good teacher will expose her students to these subjects through simple experiments, discussions, simple units and field trips. Ideally, an elementary school curriculum will also include music, art, and beginning foreign language classes, but these type of classes depend largely on a school's budget. If there is no budget for separate music and art teachers, the regular classroom teacher should incorporate these subjects into her curriculum.

To promote children's well-being, the curriculum should also include physical play, as well as basic lessons in health, hygiene, nutrition, and safety.

## Class Size

Class size is especially important from kindergarten through third grade, when children are not yet capable of working totally on their own and are trying to master the difficult task of reading. Ask the school you are considering what their maximum and minimum class size limit is. If the maximum is more than 25, you may want to consider another program for your child. Ideally, a kindergarten or first grade class should have 20 or fewer students. If the teacher has an assistant or a teacher's aide, a few more students may be manageable. Remember, the fewer students in the class, the more time the teacher will be able to spend with your child.

## The Teacher

"It is my personal approach that creates the climate. It is my daily mood that makes the weather. As a teacher, I possess tremendous power to make a child's life miserable or joyous. I can be a tool of torture or an instrument of inspiration. I can humiliate or humor, hurt or heal." So wrote the late teacher and psychologist Haim Ginott, Ph.D., in his book *Between Parent and Child* (Avon Books). Most of us in recalling our own school days would agree. Some teachers never seemed to reach out and inspire, while others seemed to care a great deal and always bring out the best in us.

If your child has a good teacher, just about all the other factors discussed in this chapter can be compromised. Here are some qualities of a good teacher.

1. A good teacher is patient and supportive. She does not ridicule a student and is quick to reinforce a tender ego with praise.
2. A good teacher teaches children how to think, not just how to spit out facts.

3. There should be discussion going on in an effective classroom, not just a teacher's monologue.

4. A good teacher roams the room to work with children on a one-to-one basis.

5. A good teacher will try a variety of techniques in teaching a difficult skill to a child who is having problems. She does not expect every child in her class to learn a skill from the same teaching method.

6. A good teacher has high expectations from ALL of the students in her class. Studies show that when teachers expect less than the best, the child's performance is often below his capabilities.

7. A good teacher will instigate activities which are not centered around her, therefore inviting children to participate and to invent projects of their own, teaching them to experiment with their thinking skills and apply what they have already learned.

8. A good teacher will maintain discipline in her classroom in a consistent manner which is not demeaning to the students. They know what is expected of them and they are aware of the consequences of bad behavior.

9. A good teacher knows that learning is fun. Her classroom is an interesting and secure place for a child to spend his day.

10. A good teacher is flexible. If one method fails, she moves effortlessly to the next. If circumstances interrupt her planned schedule, she improvises and adjusts with no problem.

11. A good teacher (especially in elementary school) has a sense of humor and uses it often.

12. A good teacher occasionally makes mistakes. Allow her this without becoming overly critical.

Your child's opinion of his teacher is almost as important as yours. In kindergarten and first grade, children tend to view the teacher as a mirror image of the parent—virtually as if the figure at the head of the classroom had all the attributes of Mother. Indeed, many kindergarten and first grade teachers will admit to having mistakenly been called "Mama" by an absorbed student.

Allan Shedlin Jr. executive director of the Elementary School Center in New York City surveyed hundreds of students to find out what they thought made up a good teacher. His findings included "someone who thought it was okay to laugh", "a person who wanted us to learn for our good, not hers", "somebody who really liked what she taught" and "somebody who didn't make us feel little, even though we were". One of the most repeated comments was "someone who is really interested in what we are saying."

So we can conclude that what a child wants in a teacher is really very similar to what parents expect. For more information on teachers, see *Tips For Dealing With Your Child's Teacher* in the next chapter.

## Specialists

Most schools employ a variety of specialists—including reading teachers, teachers of the gifted, and speech therapists—to help students with special needs. As you walk around the school, look for and ask about these special programs.

Find out what programs are available, who teaches them and what qualifications they have. Ask if the specialists have their own rooms and how well equipped they are. Many times a district will have a specialist's salary included in their budget, but her room may be a converted old broom closet with materials she has gathered on her own.

To whom are these services available? Sometimes specialists are funded by state or federal grants to help only a particular group of children. Other times, a child must demonstrate a specific need or receive a specific score on certain tests to be eligible. Find out how it works in your school.

Ask whether specialists take children out of class or work side by side with teachers in the classroom or, best of all, do some of both.

Ask whether the school has a full-time nurse. If she works part-time, who handles medical problems when she's not there? This question will be particularly important if your child suffers from asthma or some other chronic condition.

## Testing

A system which puts too much emphasis on tests should be avoided. Often these tests label a child for future grades, when the test may not be a fair indicator of a child's performance. Personal attention is a far more valuable monitoring tool to use with young children. A teacher's opinion of how a child is performing should be able to outweigh a poor test score, if necessary. Find out how much emphasis a school puts on testing concerning their promotion/retention policy. If promotion occurs solely on the basis of test performance, beware.

## Teacher Turnover Rate

Look for some continuity in the faculty. Teachers come and go every year for various reasons such as retiring, spouse transfers, pregnancy, etc., but it could be a sign of trouble if too many teachers are leaving each year. Ideally, a school will have a mixture of younger and more experienced teachers, as they both bring a variety of talents and skills from which both groups can learn from.

## The Principal

One of the best measures of an effective principal is the teachers' opinion of him. He is the leader of the team, and the more respected he is, the more his teachers seek to please him and do their job well. Teachers who do not have a supportive principal are under a great deal of stress and consequently cannot do their job as effectively as those who have the complete support of a capable principal. A good principal is interested in making his school the best possible place for learning and is involved in the daily goings-on. He roams the halls, visits the classrooms regularly, and listens to his faculty and students. He is supportive of his teachers and readily available to any teacher, parent, or student who has a question or concern. He does not spend the entire day in his office and welcomes visitors to his school. If the principal of a school fits this description, it is much more likely that the school will be a healthy learning environment for your child.

## Parents' Views

Seek out the opinion of people who have children that are already attending the school you are investigating. A good place to start would be with the PTA officers. Their names and telephone numbers should be available from the school's office. Ask them the school's greatest strengths and weaknesses. Ask what the current projects of the PTA are, which might give you an idea of what the school's needs are. Ask specific questions about the faculty and administration. If the school you are interested in does not have a parents' organization, that should raise some questions in your mind as to whether you can expect to have any influence on your child's education.

## The School Board

The fastest way to get to know the school board is by attending one of their monthly meetings which should be open to the public, except when matters of personnel or real estate are being discussed. These meetings can reveal what major problems the school system is facing, and how well the board members work together. Try to read between the lines: Are members squabbling constantly? Do they work with or against the superintendent? Are they concerned about the children, or their own power? Also, getting to know the lines of power in the administration equips interested parents to act as advocates for their children.

## Property Taxes

For parents who are considering public schools, looking at the local tax base is crucial. The key statistic to look for is assessed valuation per child, which is figured up by adding up all of the assessed property wealth within the school district and dividing the total by the enrollment. The higher this figure is, the better. These figures vary widely. When looking at state per-pupil expenditures, in 1992, these figures ranged from Utah's low of $3092 to New Jersey's high of $10,219.* A community with a high assessed valuation can accomplish its goals with relatively low tax rates for the district. Also find out the actual tax per thousand dollars of assessed valuation: If it is unduly high compared with that of neighboring districts, it could mean a financial strain for homeowners.

## The State Board of Education

In each state a department of education, headed by a commissioner or superintendent and guided by a board of education, sets policies, guidelines, and minimum standards to which every school district must adhere. It sets the minimum number of days students must attend school

---

*Source: National Education Association, Washington D.C., *Estimates of School Statistics,* annual (copyright); and unpublished data.

each year, for example, and makes decisions concerning standardized testing. A local school board cannot eliminate such testing, if it is required by the state. Sometimes there are procedures for obtaining waivers or exemptions from certain requirements if the district can demonstrate that it is meeting the state's minimum standards in another way.

States also provide a fairly substantial amount of funding to each school district. While some of this is distributed on the basis of competitive grants, most is issued according to a formula that takes into account the relative wealth of each district as well as the needs of students. There is a great deal of debate about whether these formulas are fair. Some activists believe that state monies should be used to equalize per-student spending across districts so that students in poorer areas, especially inner cities, aren't penalized by where they live. New Jersey is trying to put this into effect. This is very controversial because parents and educators in wealthier districts don't want to lose state funds which would force them to cut back their programs. Proponents of this policy believe that creating equity in educational funding is a critically important state responsibility.

Obviously, there is a lot of time and effort involved in choosing an appropriate school for your child, but you will find that it is definitely worth the extra effort. After all, if you were considering a new car purchase, you would hardly think twice about visiting several car dealerships and doing a little comparison and research. Isn't a child's education worth much more than that?

# Chapter 10

# WAYS A PARENT CAN MAKE A DIFFERENCE

Academic researchers have conducted literally hundreds of studies to confirm what common sense tells us: *Children of parents who are involved in their education demonstrate a higher level of academic achievement than children whose parents are not.* This holds true in all types of communities: rich and poor, black and white, Asian and Latino, and every other group you can think of. *Involved parents mean more successful children.* It's that simple! Here are some specific ways in which you *can* make a difference in your child's school:

1. **Offer specific help.** If you know of a need in your child's classroom such as art paper, pencils, volunteers, make an effort to fill the need. Every teacher is in need of *something.* Even if it's just a bathroom break or help grading papers.

2. **Consult teachers on fund-raisers and other "parent" projects.** It may be a great idea to raise money for new playground equipment by holding a magazine drive, but *not* if the whole effort is then handed over to the teachers to run. It also helps if parents and teachers agree in advance on the specific purpose of the funds to be raised.

3. **Learn how the social system works.** It is important for parents to begin to do things together, but approaches vary from community to community. Parent-school sports' days, picnics, exercise classes, book discussions, and potluck suppers may all be ways of getting to know one another, but they add many hours to a teacher's schedule. Teachers see school as a work place and want to live their own lives.

4. **Recognize teachers' special abilities.** You will stimulate more improvement by inviting teachers to parent meetings to describe their successes than if you sit around criticizing their shortcomings. Many teachers say, "The only time I hear from parents is when they want to complain about something." You need talented, energetic teachers to support school improvements.

5. **Work with the principal.** And keep in mind that individual principals have different administrative styles. Think about how that person

141

best responds to proposed changes, and work in a way that fits his individual style. Principals are the gatekeepers, and not much will happen without their participation.

6. **Give schools public support.** Back school budgets and needed bond votes, support improved pay for teachers, who are fast becoming the most underpaid professionals in the United States. Remember to thank teachers personally and write occasional letters to local papers and school boards commending the staff for positive changes.

7. **Seek opportunities to implement change.** Sometimes a small grant adds incentive and recognition to a community school-development effort. Other times, the opening of a school, a change in the grades assigned to a school, or perhaps a shift in leadership or the introduction of a facility such as a computer lab, may engender even greater changes within a school system.

8. **Send messages through newsletters and other media that things are happening.** Keep the school community informed of new accomplishments which can only help parent-school relations.

9. **When you must complain, do so calmly and rationally.** School administrators and teachers are much more likely to want to work towards a solution to a problem if you are calm and rational when you explain the problem. Harsh words and displays of temper only serve to harm the relationship between you and the school and more importantly, between your child and his teacher. Whenever possible, offer a solution with your complaint.

10. **Work together toward shared planning.** Parents and staff should work toward comprehensive goals that will enhance not only the school and the learning environment but the community as well.

11. **Attend school functions.** Your attendance conveys the message that you support your child and the school and appreciate the time and effort that goes into each event.

12. **Read everything sent home from your child's school or district.** It's important to be well informed. Learn about the school's expectations and requirements. Both you and your child will feel more secure when you understand the rules and routines of her school.

## TIPS ON DEALING WITH YOUR CHILD'S TEACHER

Next to his parents, a child's teacher is perhaps the most important person in his life. In many cases, the child actually spends more waking hours with his teacher than with his parents. Your child will benefit immensely from knowing that his parents and the person who cares for him during the week respect and like each other. The little extra effort it takes to build this kind of partnership with your child's teacher will make your child feel more secure and will reap many rewards for your child. For starters, keep these points in mind:

1. **It's the little things that count.** Nobody likes to be taken for granted. So don't forget ordinary courtesies like always greeting your child's teacher in the morning, or when you pick him up in the afternoon.

2. **Accentuate the positive.** Build up your child's teacher, don't knock her down. Let her know you understand that working all day with children is tiring and stressful. This acknowledgement of her dedication will make her feel appreciated, and that feeling will translate into added enjoyment of her job. When she feels happy about her work, her joy will be contagious and your child will benefit. Don't be one of the many parents who only communicate with the teacher to complain. Take time out at the end of the year or a holiday to write her a note thanking her for all of her hard work.

3. **Show your interest.** Ask specific questions about how your child is doing. Asking for particular information gives the teacher a chance to reflect about a child's development. If she didn't notice what your son did today, she will surely notice tomorrow and that will bring her into closer touch with your child.

4. **Tell her what's going on at home.** Don't hold back family news that may affect your child's behavior. Inform the teacher about any important emotional signals you receive. If you are going through a divorce or are raising a child alone, these are relevant points concerning your child's development. Alerting the teacher will help her to be more sensitive to your child's needs. But be certain you never discuss these situations in front of your child. Take the teacher aside and talk confidentially.

5. **Plan to meet and talk.** Make sure that you have a "formal" conference with your child's teacher at least twice a year. (Initiate this meeting if she doesn't ask for it.) These planned conferences, in addition to your daily contacts, give you and the teacher a chance to think about your child's development and offer an opportunity to smooth out any rough spots that exist. Find out how the school wants you to make appointments with the teacher. Most schools have specific procedures for this. Kindergarten and first grade teachers are always amazed at the number of

children whose parents never even bother to meet their child's first schoolteacher.

6. **Be honest about your child's shortcomings.** If there is something that your child does or doesn't do that bothers you, tell the teacher about it. Chances are the behavior will try her patience too. If a teacher is aware of any problems *beforehand* she is better equipped to deal with them and offer solutions to bring about change. Conversely, if your child's teacher is the one to point out a shortcoming, don't be defensive, she is not trying to be critical. It is her job to help your child become the best that he can be. Many times the teacher is the one best able to help a child overcome a shortcoming, simply because she has the ability to be more objective than a parent. Do remember that no child is perfect; each one needs some help growing up.

7. **Be discreet.** If you have a gripe about your child's teacher, don't talk about it in front of your child. You could cause him to worry unnecessarily. Though your complaint seems slight to you, it could seem substantial to your young child. When children don't understand exactly what an adult means, they make their own sense out of the words they hear. You might have said, "Miss Spalding keeps losing things—first it was your jacket and now it's your gloves. It drives me crazy!" But your child may have heard, "Miss Spalding might lose me and Mommy will be crazy!" Better to air your grievances to the teacher, in a kind tactful way—out of your child's hearing. Remember that teachers have many more opportunities to make mistakes than most of us do. A day of substitute teaching will prove to you how difficult and grueling a teacher's day can be. Children should be taught to respect their teacher and school.

8. **Don't expect to just "drop in for a minute" and talk to the teacher.** She is responsible for too many children to just drop everything and have an unplanned conference, even for just a few moments. And while a teacher stands at the door to have a minute discussion with a parent, her class often sees it as a time to lose control. Once this occurs, it can cause an otherwise smooth day to get off to a very rocky start. It is always better to send a note explaining the question, or asking the teacher to call you at her convenience. If this is not adequate, most teachers have planning time between the hour school is out and the time they leave school. Try calling at this time rather than calling a teacher at home. Just as you would not like to receive a work-related call during your off time, neither does a teacher.

According to the National Education Association, teachers work an average of ten hours per week without pay on school-related business and activities. Although she is very concerned with her students and their welfare, she has a private life that deserves your respect.

**9. Remember, teachers are only human.** If you are critical, unkind, or rude to your child's teacher, she may develop an unconscious resentment towards your child. Resist the temptation to speak your mind and lose your temper. Speak calmly and tactfully and try to see the situation from the teacher's point of view.

Taking time to practice some or all of the above suggestions can make all the difference in the world in how your child feels about school.

## THE PARENT-TEACHER CONFERENCE

Here are some questions to ask your child's teacher that will give you a good idea of how he is *really* doing in school:

- How do you see my child's work compared with expectations for the grade level? (Is he at, above, or below grade level?)
- How is my child doing in comparison with his classmates?
- Is my child working up to his full potential?
- What reading and math groups is my child in? How did you determine this and does he have an opportunity to move to another group if his work improves?
- Has my child taken any standardized tests? If so, what strengths and or weaknesses were revealed?
- How does my child get along with his classmates?
- Does he seem interested and eager in class or timid and shy?
- Is he a leader of a follower?
- What can I do specifically at home to help my child do better in school?

End your conference by telling the teacher any information that you feel might help her deal more effectively with your child. ("Charlie does well if you tell him first what you expect from him" or "Martha is shy but she would love it if you would call on her more often.")

# Chapter 11

# A LOOK AT THE KINDERGARTEN
# AND FIRST GRADE CURRICULUM

## A DEVELOPMENTALLY APPROPRIATE KINDERGARTEN

Studies show that young children learn best through hands-on practical experience. They gather meaning by doing—by manipulating objects, by experimenting with them, by hands on interaction.

A developmentally appropriate kindergarten curriculum will allow for a flexibly structured school day and will accommodate a wide range of skills and needs. The atmosphere will be cooperative, not competitive, and focus on learning through play.

*Hands-on-activities* are basic to the curriculum: Blocks of different sizes and shapes can help teach math concepts; a science lesson can involve growing and tending plants in the classroom. Many activities integrate lessons in a number of subject areas. A group activity such as baking muffins could teach math, science, reading, and social skills.

*The language arts* are central to learning in the primary grades, and one of the teacher's main goals will be to encourage a love of reading and writing. Teachers will read to children and acquaint them with a rich variety of stories, rhymes, and plays. Kindergartners should be encouraged to make up their own stories—first to dictate them to the teacher and illustrate them, and later to write their stories themselves, using invented or transitional spelling.

The development of language skills happens in all subject areas. Learning basic math terms, for instance, builds a child's vocabulary; in social studies, listening to a story about a family in another country develops listening skills and helps prepare a child to read herself.

*Fostering curiosity, imagination, and self-expression* will all be important goals. In music or drawing class, the emphasis will be on enjoyment rather than criticism. Teachers will applaud the creativity of beginning writers.

*Social skills* are developed in kindergarten as children learn to take turns

146

speaking during class discussions, for example, to share toys and materials, and to cooperate with one another on classroom projects.

*A sense of social responsibility* and ideas about good citizenship begin to form when a child learns, for example, in science class about the importance of protecting the environment, or in social studies about significant historical figures and their contributions to society.

*To promote children's well-being,* kindergarten will include time for active physical play, as well as basic lessons in health, hygiene, nutrition, and safety.

## WHAT YOU SHOULD KNOW ABOUT PRESCHOOL TESTING

There are two kinds of tests your preschooler may face: a school-readiness test and an IQ test. Parents should be aware of the differences and know which test their child is taking.

### Readiness Tests

Readiness tests are sometimes a component of the admissions process of special programs and independent schools. However, they are more often used to place a child already at school in an appropriate program for his abilities and to determine whether he may have any special needs.

**Gesell Developmental Observation Kindergarten Assessment.** This test is most commonly used for kindergarten placement. It is a subjective test, meaning there are no right or wrong answers. A child's behavior during the test is as important as her performance. Test time: usually 20 to 30 minutes. Children are asked to build with blocks, to draw, and to discuss their favorite activities, among other things.

**Metropolitan Readiness Tests—Fifth Edition.** Level I can be given to children at the beginning of kindergarten. It tests letter recognition, visual matching, auditory memory, and quantitative language, listening, and sound matching skills. Level II can be given to children at the end of kindergarten or in first grade. Each level takes 80 to 100 minutes and is usually given in two separate sessions.

## IQ Tests

IQ tests are commonly required for entrance to private schools and to some public school programs, although some states have banned them for use in public schools. The tests usually take about an hour but can go longer, since the test giver does not stop until a child begins to answer a number of items incorrectly. On the Wechsler and Stanford-Binet tests, some of the units are timed.

**Wechsler Preschool and Primary Scale of Intelligence—Revised.** Given to children between the ages of three and seven and a half, this Wechsler test, often given for private school admission because of its breakdown of scores for each subtest, emphasizes visual, verbal, and motor skills. Twelve subtest are divided into a verbal scale and a performance scale. IQs are reported for each individual scale and are then combined to compute the full-scale IQ. Parents are provided with a written analysis of the child's performance on the various subtests and are told the IQ *range*—average, bright-normal, superior, very superior, or gifted.

**Wechsler Intelligence Scale for Children—Revised.** This test is similar to the WPPSI–R but is given to children between ages six and seventeen.

**Raven's Colored Progressive Matrices.** This nonverbal exam for children ages five to eleven assesses reasoning skills by requiring children to figure out color sequences and patterns.

**Stanford-Binet Intelligence Scale—Fourth Edition.** The first intelligence test to be widely used in this country, the Stanford-Binet is geared to measuring reasoning and memory skills. The test items are similar to those on the Wechslers. A child is asked questions until he gets a certain percentage of them wrong, which provides a means of assessing cognitive ability. Parents will be told their child's ability range in comparison to those of other students in the same nation, but they are never given a specific number because numbers can label a child.

## How Parents Can Help

A child should have a routine physical, dental, and eye exam just prior to taking the test in order to make sure that physiological problems are not responsible for any poor test results. Make sure your child is well rested the day of the test. If for some reason your child becomes very upset before going to the test, you should consider postponing it.

The most essential ingredient in achieving an accurate score is child-

and-tester rapport, a bond that should be established before the test begins.

Tell your child that she is going to meet a person like her nursery school teacher who will ask her some questions and want her to do some drawings or puzzles or play with blocks. Mention that these activities will take place in a special room and that you will be in the waiting room. She should know that some of her answers will be wrong and that it's okay if they are.

Under optimum conditions children are often not even aware they are being tested. They see it as a game or play time.

Above all, parents should project a sense of calm. If a child is nervous, most often it's because her parent is nervous too, testers say.

### Should You Prep Your Child Before the Test?

Any one with a little ingenuity can find a copy of the test, but a parent can do her child perhaps no greater disservice than to try to prep her, say experts, because the plan is almost sure to backfire.

Testers say that prepping usually shows up on the test, then the child gets a comment on the evaluation that says there was some prior exposure to the material. Schools don't look upon this favorably.

But the bottom line is that it's unfair to the child to place her in a program in which the challenge is beyond her abilities. There's too much emphasis these days on "gifted" programs and the "best" schools. The emphasis should be on finding the *appropriate* school.

Above all, it's best not to put too much faith in a form of testing that is at best limited and, by many standards, outdated. Parents should accept both the narrowness of the judgment and the short-term nature of its prognostications. You should also follow your instincts as a parent when you sense something has gone wrong in the testing procedure. Parents know their children better than any test does. If you have reason to believe the test is not an accurate reflection of your child's abilities, make inquiries, because you're probably right.

### POSTPONING KINDERGARTEN?

Some parents decide to hold back their child from entering kindergarten, believing that it's better to wait than to flunk. They feel their child needs another year at home or in a preschool program before entering the public school system and may decide on their own to wait a year. In most states, parents have the legal right to do this.

## Some Good Reasons

Factors that influence such parental decisions might be a child's relative immaturity compared with peers, family stress that might indicate the child needs an extra year of nurturing at home, and knowledge of a particular kindergarten's curriculum. If the available program is known to be more like the first grade than kindergarten, an extra year of development at home or in an age-appropriate early childhood program may well be a gift to a child. If, however, the kindergarten has an age appropriate curriculum taught by skilled, nurturing teachers (the ideal situation), most experts agree that there's no need to withhold a child. On the contrary, they say, such a kindergarten will be highly beneficial for even the youngest child in the class.

## Some Not-So-Good Reasons

These days, a sad phenomenon is becoming increasingly common, particularly among fast-track parents. Some are deliberately keeping back children who *are* actually ready for kindergarten, believing that if their child is one of the oldest in the group when he finally does start school, he will be ahead both academically and in terms of his physical development. And while this supposition may hold true for the first few years of a child's school experience, the retention sometimes backfires when the child reaches the upper grades. Such children are both bigger and more socially mature than the others in their grade level and may end up feeling out of step with their younger classmates.

## A KINDERGARTEN READINESS CHECKLIST

In a survey conducted by D. Keith Osborn, a professor of child development and education at the University of Georgia, more than 3,000 kindergarten teachers in the United States and Canada were asked to list what skills children need in order to be ready for entering kindergarten. While Osborn stresses that your child does not need to master every one of these skills, the following is a sampling of what teachers think a beginning kindergartner should be able to do:

- Sit and focus for some length of time (5 or more minutes at first, 20 or more later on).
- Listen to directions.
- Follow simple rules.
- Get dressed by himself.
- Button or zipper his jacket.
- Tie or Velcro his shoes.
- Use a toilet and wash up.
- Know parents' names, home address, and phone number.
- Remember objects from a picture.
- Use a pair of scissors correctly.
- Color and trace an object.
- Blow his nose with a tissue.
- Identify common farm and zoo animals.
- Recognize primary colors.
- Recognize circle, square, triangle, and rectangle.
- Understand the differences between concepts such as empty and full, hot and cold, and up and down.
- Build with blocks.
- Put away all of his things after using them.
- Demonstrate an ability to get along well with others.
- Share and take turns.
- Work independently.
- Function away from a parent for more than two to three hours a day.
- Can repeat number sequence (ex: 264, 4285, 93175).
- Uses descriptive language.
- Follows oral directions.
- Gives appropriate answers to questions.
- Prints first name.
- Can say first and last name.
- Can give birthday.
- Identifies numbers 0–10.
- Counts to ten.
- Counts items in a set.
- Identifies at least 13 letters of the alphabet.
- Identifies body parts such as eye, wrist, elbow, right hand, back, ear, shoulder, knee, ankle, left leg.
- Can reproduce a circle, square, rectangle, and triangle.
- Can jump, hop on one foot, skip, and walk a straight line.

- When drawing a man, the following are included: head, ears, eyes, nose, mouth, hair, arms, hand and fingers, body, legs, feet, clothes.
- Holds a book right side up.
- Turns pages from left to right.

## BASIC KINDERGARTEN INSTRUCTIONAL OBJECTIVES

Keep in mind, there are no federal guidelines for kindergarten curriculums and some states do not even require public kindergarten. For this reason, the objectives of any given kindergarten program will vary greatly, but these serve as a *general* example of what a child is expected to learn in kindergarten.

### Reading and Readiness

The student will:

1. Retell a story in own words.
2. Tell story with beginning, middle and end.
3. Enjoy listening to stories.
4. Sequence events in an orally presented story.
5. Recognize details in an orally presented story.
6. Recognize main idea in an orally presented story.
7. Follow oral directions.
8. Identify spoken words with the same beginning sound.
9. Identify spoken words with the same ending sounds.
10. Identify spoken rhyming words.

### Beginning Reading

11. Match like written letters.
12. Match like written words.
13. Recognize and name uppercase alphabet letters.
14. Recognize and name lowercase alphabet letters.
15. Match uppercase letters to lowercase letters.
16. Recognize own first and last name in print.
17. Read simple words.
18. Read simple sentences.
19. Read simple stories with assistance.

## Writing

The student will:

### Composition

1. Write his/her own name in manuscript.
2. Arrange a group of three pictures in an appropriate sequential pattern.
3. Classify objects according to color clues.
4. Describe an event which he or she has seen or experienced.
5. Understand the difference between a question and statement and respond appropriately.
6. Demonstrate an understanding of positional prepositions and adverbs (i.e., above, below, on, etc.).
7. Express orally correct plural forms of nouns, using "s."
8. Express orally correct possessive forms of nouns, adding "s".

### Language and Mechanics

1. Demonstrate hand-eye coordination in nonwriting tasks.
2. Holding writing implement correctly.
3. Place paper correctly for writing.
4. Sit in correct writing position.
5. Given models, draw lines demonstrating the concept of top to bottom.
6. Given models, draw lines demonstrating the concept of left to right.
7. Given models, form basic shapes needed in manuscript.
8. Given models, form lowercase letters.
9. Given models, form uppercase letters.
10. Given models, form the numerals 0–9.

### Mathematics

**Cluster I**

1. Identify positions: over, above, up, between, etc.
2. Compare length: nearer, nearest, etc.
3. Compare area; volume: more, less, smaller(est), larger(est).

### Cluster II

4. Compare sets: equal, not equal in number, <5.
5. Compare sets: more, less; pictured objects, <5.
6. Read numbers and count: numerals and sets 0–5.
7. Identify positions: first, last, before, after, etc.

### Cluster III

8. Compare size; shape: same, different.
9. Identify figures: circle, triangle, rectangle, square.
10. Complete pattern: by size or shape.
11. Order events: first, last, next.

### Cluster IV

12. Read numbers and count: numerals and sets, 0–10.
13. Count: 1–10.
14. Read numbers: 0–10.
15. Count money: pennies, < 9 cents.

### Cluster V

16. Compare numbers: more than, less than; numerals < 10.
17. Compare numbers: larger(est), smaller(est), greater(est), < 10.
18. Compare capacity: empty, more, less, etc.
19. Compare mass: lighter, heavier.

### Cluster VI

20. Add: match addition statements to pictures, < 10.
21. Subtract: match subtraction statements to pictures, < 10.
22. Compare sets: how many extra (more), pictured objects, < 10.
23. Interpret problems, plus (+) or minus (−); oral stories for pictures, < 10.

## FIRST GRADE INSTRUCTIONAL OBJECTIVES

As each state is responsible for writing and developing its own curriculum, learning objectives may vary greatly. This list is intended to be a *general* guide to what a first grade child may be taught. Only language arts and math are covered here, but a complete curriculum would include science, social studies, music, art, and physical education.

## Language Arts

The student will:

1. Use a variety of language patterns and sentence structures.
2. Retell stories read, heard or viewed.
3. Distinguish between letter/word, word/sentence, left/right, beginning/ending of words and sentences.
4. Demonstrate an understanding that the purpose of reading is to obtain/gain meaning from print.
5. Reread for understanding.
6. Recognize explicit and implicit main ideas, details, sequence of events, and cause-effect relationships.
7. Make predictions in a story.
8. Identify the main character in a story.
9. Classifies and categorizes words.
10. Recognizes auditory similarities and differences in words including beginning and ending sounds.
11. Uses word families and sound-letter relationships of consonants and single vowels in word recognition.
12. Identifies grade level vocabulary by sight.
13. Recalls a series of four visually presented items.
14. Participates in prewriting, drafting, revising, and publishing a story.
15. Begins editing for capitalization and punctuation.
16. Expands writing vocabulary.
17. Dictates and writes creative stories using descriptive language.
18. Uses pictures, words, and inventive spelling in personal writing.
19. Expresses ideas in sentence form.
20. Prints numerals and letters legibly.
21. Demonstrates an interest in various types of literature.
22. Answers literal, inferential, and critical questions about literature.
23. Recognizes literary forms: fiction/nonfiction, poetry.
24. Discriminates between realism and fantasy.
25. Uses picture dictionaries, easy fiction and nonfiction books, and various audiovisual software as information sources.
26. Recognizes the author, illustrator and title as identifying items of information about a book.
27. Recognizes the purpose of the title page and the table of contents.
28. Alphabetizes words to the first letter.

## Math

The student will:

1. Select concrete objects belonging or not belonging to a given set.
2. Recognize equivalent and nonequivalent sets.
3. Models whole numbers through 99 using groups of tens and ones and orally names numbers (e.g., 3 tens, 2 ones or thirty-two).
4. Selects the numeral that names a group of objects and matches a group of objects with the appropriate numeral.
5. Recognizes, writes and orally names numerals 0–99.
6. Translates words to numerals and numerals to words (0–10).
7. Identifies number of tens and ones in a given number.
8. Identifies place value through tens.
9. Identifies a specified positional relationship between objects (before, after, between, near, close to).
10. Identifies numerical relations (greater than, less than, equal to) of numbers 0–99 and sequences numbers in ascending order.
11. Uses ordinal numbers first through ninth to indicate position.
12. Uses appropriate mathematical symbols: $+$, $-$, $=$.
13. Recognizes different ways of representing fractions using concrete and picture models and words for one-half, one-third, and one-fourth.
14. Determines the cardinal number for a given set (0–100).
15. Identifies circles, squares, triangles, and rectangles of various types and in various orientations.
16. Identifies balls, cubes, and cones.
17. Identifies geometric relations (larger, largest, smaller, smallest, same size, same shape, inside, outside, on, left, right).
18. Compares weight of two real objects (heavier, lighter) and capacity of two real containers (more, less).
19. Selects appropriate units (minutes, hours, days, weeks, months) and appropriate instruments (clocks) to measure time.
20. Identifies days, weeks, and months on a calendar.
21. Identifies number of minutes in an hour, number of hours in a day, and number of days in a week.
22. Identifies coins and bills (penny, nickel, dime, quarter, one dollar, and five dollars).
23. Explores addition and subtraction with words pictures and con-

crete models, particularly sums to 18 and related differences, and multiples of ten.

24. Determines addition facts (sums to 18) and related subtraction facts using strategies such as counting all of a set, part/part/whole, counting on, counting back, counting up, doubles, property of zero, and commutativity of addition.
25. Recalls addition facts (sums to 10) and related subtraction facts.
26. Determines the value of a set of coins up to 25 — using nickels, pennies and dimes and quarters.
27. Tells time to half hour and hour.
28. Measures length using inch and centimeter.
29. Counts by ones, twos, fives, and tens to 100. Counts back from 12.
30. Continues simple patterns such as those involving numbers, shapes, colors, and so forth.
31. Constructs simple graphs using concrete objects, blocks, or squares.
32. Interprets data by reading bar graphs and pictographs using whole unit data.
33. Writes a number sentence that describes a given story problem or problem situation.

# Chapter 12

# QUESTIONS ABOUT YOUR CHILD'S SCHOOL

*What exactly is meant by the term "whole language"?*

Like many educational terms, whole-language learning means different things in different schools. The basic idea is that from the start, children are encouraged to acquire and expand their language skills through a combination of related reading, writing, and speaking activities. Instead of being taught how to read through a standard reading text and accompanying workbook, children are introduced to regular books and are encouraged to see the study of literature as a gratifying reason to learn how to read. Children are also encouraged to write their own stories early, often first by dictating them to adults and then by writing words, even when they have no spelling skills. Children are urged to engage in frequent discussions with one another and their parents about their reading and writing. Most early elementary school teachers have always relied on this approach to an extent, but there are some significant differences today.

A whole language approach plays down, or even eliminates traditional reading texts. Experienced teachers say that this approach stresses comprehension, quickens children's interest in literature, and gets them reading real books earlier than a structured method would. The risk is that some of the basics, such as phonics instruction may be missed by less seasoned teachers who are not familiar with methods of incorporating phonics into reading instruction.

Educators are working hard to ensure that the whole-language approach does not become just another educational fad; it is a creative way to develop a love of reading and pride in writing well.

*Is phonics instruction the cure for my son's reading problem?*

Despite the publicity accorded books promoting phonics, it is not a cure-all. Phonics is simply the part of the reading process in which letters or letter groups are associated with sounds. A good reading program will include phonics in the instruction of reading, but learning to read is much more complicated than that. There are perhaps half a dozen components involved in the process of learning to read, and each reinforces the other. If phonics alone could do the trick, reading difficulties would have vanished years ago when the concept first came into vogue.

The following often play a part in reading problems:

*Physical factors.* Any type of visual or auditory handicap will make reading more difficult. Temporary hearing problems caused by earlier ear infections can have lasting effects because the child may have missed important early experience in sound discrimination.

*Emotional factors.* It is obvious that children who have deep psychological problems will find learning hard, but so will children who are worried about a loved one's illness, the possibility of moving to a new community, or a parental divorce.

*Educational deficiencies.* Children with an impoverished language background, who have not been read to and who cannot relate word use to concrete experiences and objects during the preschool years, are at a disadvantage. Similarly, educational approaches to reading that are too narrow can deprive children of the skills they need.

*Language-processing and brain functioning problems.* Some children cannot readily put together the pieces of language because of how their brain functions. A child's difficulties can be easily discerned by reading-language therapists, but their causes and cure are the subject of major research efforts in the relatively new field of neurobiology.

*Sex differences.* It is well established that boys have a harder time with early reading than girls do. The causes—whether developmental, neurological, or cultural—are the subject of heated debate and much research.

You should seek the advice of your child's teacher or, if necessary, specialists at a reading clinic. Then work with the school to establish a suitable remedial program rather than spend your money on what may be an inappropriate strategy.

**My child's teacher suspects that my son is learning disabled and has requested permission to have him tested. What does all of this mean?**

Two million school age children have been labeled learning disabled (LD). Children with learning disabilities may have problems listening, thinking, talking, reading, writing, spelling or doing arithmetic. Although LD children are enormously different from one another, in each case there is a disorder that inhibits learning.

Learning disabilities are believed to be brain dysfunctions that delay the normal learning process for one or more cognitive abilities. Learning disabilities are not the result of poor vision, poor hearing, a motor handicap such as cerebral palsy, or an emotional disturbance such as a parent's divorce. Nor are learning disabilities related to cultural or economic disadvantages.

A child may have difficulty interpreting what he sees, or he may not be able to remember what he has heard. The problem lies not in *receiving* information but in *processing* it. Most learning disabled children are of normal or above-average intelligence, and some are even gifted. It is this sad discrepancy between a child's potential and his achievement that targets him as learning disabled.

LD children often exhibit other behaviors aside from poor school performance, such as clumsiness, poor memory, and a limited attention span. Sometimes these problems are a direct result of the learning disability; other times they are manifestations of the emotional problems of children who are "failures" in school. Many have low self-esteem and difficulty making friends.

What is the cause of learning disabilities? Although there is no single cause, there is growing evidence that some particular types of learning disabilities may have a genetic origin. Other risk factors beginning in pregnancy include poor maternal nutrition, alcoholism or substance abuse, or diseases such as German measles. All of these could affect fetal brain size and body size. During birth infants may experience oxygen loss, premature delivery, or damage from medical instruments. Other risk factors include environmental deprivation, such as inadequate or improper nutrition or sensory and psychological stimulation.

A learning disability is not a disease. There is no cure. Learning disabilities are generally not outgrown. But with proper education affected children can learn to compensate for their disabilities and live normal lives, especially once their school years are behind them. Helping children attain an appropriate education and a positive self-image is primarily a parental responsibility.

If you suspect a problem during your child's preschool years, keep in mind that no two children develop at the same rate. Then trust your intuition.

Preschoolers who display some of the following behaviors are generally too young to be labeled learning disabled but may be at risk for developmental problems:

- significantly delayed language development
- continual, nondirected activity
- short attention span
- delayed motor skills
- poor memory skills
- difficulty with other children

When a child is *consistently* slower in developing skills, an evaluation may be helpful. But it is also possible that the child is just developmentally slow.

It is extremely important to identify a preschooler with problems because the sooner a child gets help, the better his chances of developing properly. An evaluation can also help in deciding if early remediation is needed.

If your child is having problems in one or more academic subjects, or is feeling under stress at school, you should suspect a problem. The teacher's observation may lead to a recommendation for an evaluation. A child who is not reading by the end of the first grade is cause for alarm. Teachers who suspect a learning disability look for various indicators:

- difficulty with reading, spelling, written expression, or math
- poor concentration
- difficulty remembering
- problems with organization
- apathy and indifference
- hostility toward schoolwork

If you think your child's ability to learn is being impeded by some form of disability, you should seek an assessment, which every school is required by law to provide. Request the assessment in writing and keep a copy for your files.

Assessments are somewhat varied, but the rudimentary components will ideally include meetings with a school psychologist, a social worker, and an educational specialist.

The purpose of an assessment is to understand a child's strengths and needs so that a specific educational package can be created to suit his individual learning style. It usually consists of a battery of several tests:

- A measure of IQ, the numerical ratio of a child's learning potential in comparison with other children the same age (within a three to six month range). For the diagnosis of learning disability to be made, a discrepancy between ability and school achievement *must* be demonstrated.

- Achievement tests. These determine at which grade level the child is functioning in the areas of reading, written language, and math.
- An assessment of the child's skills in oral language, motor development, and other nonverbal skills.
- A measure of the child's strengths and weaknesses in learning. This indicator will help determine how the child learns best. Discovering *how* a particular child learns is crucial in drawing up an educational plan.
- Classroom observation.
- Conversations with parents and teachers regarding the child's behavioral development.

Depending on where the child is assessed and the nature of his problems, the evaluation might also include medical, neurological, and psychological testing. A *single* test or observation is never sufficient.

Even though a child may not be performing well in school, he will not be diagnosed as learning disabled if his test results are near grade level or if another causal condition is found. The term "learning disabled" applies *only* to a child who performs significantly below par in one or more areas of learning tested.

After the evaluation is completed, a meeting is held to share the test results with the parents. Although these meetings can be intimidating, this is the parent's opportunity to ask questions and make sure that they understand their child's problem. If you feel uneasy about the school's findings, you can seek another assessment from a private agency. Sometimes insurance will cover some or all of the cost of the outside evaluation.

Completing the assessment is only the first step in helping a learning disabled child. If it is determined that the child does qualify as learning disabled, the school will develop an Individualized Educational Plan (IEP). The IEP includes both long- and short-term educational goals for the child. It is up to the parent to approve or disapprove the plan.

The IEP will recommend that the child be placed in special education classes, or a special school. It must state the reasons for each recommendation as well as list alternatives. The IEP strives to place the student in the least restrictive special education program, often allowing participation in some mainstream classes. The goal is always to move the child as quickly as possible into a less restrictive environment.

There are many ways parents can ensure the best educational program for their learning disabled child. The ideal is to strive for a working alliance with the parent and the school. Here are some suggestions:

- Remember that you are your child's most important advocate. Be tough.
- Learn all you can about learning disabilities. There are several addresses listed in the appendix of this book that can help.
- Remember that under federal law, all children have the right to a free and appropriate education. Your school is obligated to assess your child every three years, review his IEP at least once a year, and provide necessary support services. In addition, you must be given written notice before the school takes any action on your child's behalf. You have the right to be involved in planning for your child's education.
- Keep careful, organized records, along with copies of all correspondence. Keep evaluations, IEP's, and other information. You are also legally entitled to see your child's school records. Request these from the school principal.
- Get involved with the school. Be supportive whenever possible. Meet with the teachers to discuss your child's differences in a nonthreatening way. Let them know they can always contact you if they have any concerns.

Perhaps the most important point is to realize what a crucial role you play in your child's opinion of himself. These suggestions are for helping a learning disabled child *at home.*

- Emphasize your child's strengths. Find *something* your child does well and praise him often.
- Discuss the learning disability with your child *and* the whole family. Often a child's fantasies about his problem can be far worse than reality. By making the disability a fact of family life, the problem loses much of its mystery and stigma. Be accepting and encourage family members to do the same.
- Acknowledge your child's frustrations. Let him know that you understand his difficulties. Then deal with what your child *can* do. A child who is confident about his verbal abilities may tell a teacher, "*Ask* me the questions. I can't write well, but I know this stuff!"
- Find your child's style of learning and help him use it at home. If a

child learns well visually, *show* him what you want him to do instead of barking orders at him.

- Keep discipline short, immediate, and appropriate. Children with learning problems often have difficulty understanding cause and effect. Help them understand why they are being punished.

- Give each child in the family what he needs. Fairness is a matter of meeting each child's individual needs. Recognize the different needs and wants of each child.

- Read *Mothers Talk About Learning Disabilities* (Prentice Hall), by Elizabeth Weiss, the mother of two learning disabled boys.

- Accept your child just the way he is. Love him and tell him he is special often.

### *I suspect my child may be intellectually gifted. What is the best way to prove my suspicions?*

As unreliable as many experts claim it is, the IQ test seems to be the across-the-board choice for identifying gifted children. Estimates are that it is being used as the primary barometer for identifying giftedness in more than 90 percent of the programs today. Indeed, more than 40 states currently require or recommend an IQ test for this purpose.

The debate over gifted children has been confounded in recent years by the profusion of classes for preschoolers—such as swimming, computers, music, and foreign languages—that claim to give children a competitive edge. The child who is fluent in French by age four is hailed as gifted; likewise a 4 year old who swims Olympic length laps. This is simply not true, experts insist. Most of the evidence tells us that this early kind of pushing can do emotional damage, and by the time they reach third grade, these children are no more ahead than children who were not pushed.

Most of the research says that parents generally do not know when they have a gifted child. Some of the indicators parents can be on the lookout for include an uncanny appreciation of the life around them. Gifted children look at things with a particular alertness, they have a good memory, and they spot subtleties. Perhaps one of the more endearing indicators is a sense of humor. When you comprehend a joke you are recognizing an incongruity.

One of the best ways in which a parent can determine if a child is advanced or not is to make comparisons with his peers. Gifted children do things a little earlier, a little faster, a little differently and maybe a little better than most children.

The first thing parents who think they have a gifted child should do is to carefully cultivate any emerging interests *without* applying pressure. The three year old who enjoys plunking away on the piano for extended periods of time, for example, has demonstrated an interest in and perhaps an affinity for music. That child should probably be exposed to something musical. It can be formal instruction or just exposure to different music. That parent would be satisfying an appetite, yet not forcing a child to take an interest in something he doesn't understand, or finds boring.

At this tender age, putting even the genuinely gifted child through the paces of an exhaustive schedule of classes and pushing him to learn and accomplish may do more harm than good. Too high expectations can make children feel they have had it by the time they get to elementary school. That is the greater danger. Too much is expected of them, and as a result, they're deprived of their childhoods.

Unfortunately, not all public schools offer gifted programs at the grade school level. According to the National Center for Education Statistics in Washington, D.C., only 25 states currently mandate special programs for the gifted and talented. Parents should lobby for a program in their school by contacting the local Board of Education or their State Commission on Education.

Private education opportunities for gifted children are sometimes more prolific. Families who don't have access to a public school program may want to explore such possibilities for just as the overstimulated child will turn off, so will the understimulated one.

Some good news: the federal Department of Education has just awarded a $7.5 million grant for the funding of a new National Research Center on the Gifted and Talented to be based at the University of Connecticut at Storrs. Their aim: to develop new methods of identification and instruction for talented and gifted children.

**My child's teacher referred to his "permanent record" during a conference. What information is included here?**

A permanent record card is started when a child enters kindergarten and follows him until he graduates from high school. If he leaves the school district, a copy is usually sent to his new school. The card contains such things as end-of-the-year grades, attendance and health records, standardized test scores, teacher comments, reports and recommendations to staff from school support personnel, honors and special recognitions, and disciplinary actions.

In 1974 our right to review our children's permanent records and to challenge any unfair or inaccurate comments in them was legislated by the Freedom of Information Act, which is part of the federal Family Educational Rights and Privacy Act. This act also prohibits the school from releasing student records to other agencies or institutions without your permission.

### What is the difference between standardized, norm-referenced and criterion-referenced tests?

A test is *standardized* if it is given to a large number of people under roughly the same conditions. Most school systems give standardized tests every year beginning in the second grade to measure students' achievement in reading and math.

Most standardized tests given to our children in school are *norm-referenced;* that is, they compare each child's score to a norm or the scores of other children of the same age who have already taken the test. The comparison is usually expressed in a percentile score. A child scoring at the eightieth percentile, for example, had more correct answers than 80 percent of other children on her grade level; 20 percent of them had more correct answers than she did. Norm-referenced tests are based on the assumption that scores should fall along a bell-shaped or normal curve. Norm-referenced tests give a small number of students very high or very low scores; most students fall in the center. Critics of standardized tests question this practice, pointing out that the distribution of human abilities and knowledge doesn't necessarily fall along a bell-shaped curve.

In contrast, almost everyone who takes a *criterion-referenced* test could, in theory, pass it. The written test we take to get a driver's license is an example. Our scores are not compared with others. The test simply measures whether or not we have mastered the material and our scores reflect our correct answers. Most of the spelling and math tests that your child takes in elementary school will be criterion-referenced.

### What should I do if my child does not like his teacher?

Initially it will take around six weeks before your child is totally comfortable and adjusted to his new teacher and likewise for the teacher. However, keep in mind that sometimes a child will go through phases where he is not as fond of his teacher as usual. The reasons for this range from the fact that the teacher is introducing a new skill which the child is having trouble with, to not being selected helper of the week. I often jokingly tell parents, "I won't believe what Laura says about you, if you won't believe what she says about me." In any case, encourage your child to talk about his feelings towards his teacher and try to determine the cause of them. If the problem persists, make arrangements to meet with the teacher and discuss the problem. Try to work together to come up with a solution. Often times, the child is overly sensitive in a particular area and all that is needed to correct the problem is to call the teacher's attention to this fact. Don't just assume that the problem will go away or get better on its own. Remember that your child's attitude concerning school and his teacher is being formed for the rest of his elementary school years and it is your responsibility to see that it is an appropriate one.

*I have been told by neighbors that my child's teacher is one of the weaker ones in the school. What should I do?*

Often rumors about a teacher get started and last for many years. More often than not they are based on vague impressions or the bad experience of a particular child. While it is true that teachers differ in their teaching styles and methods, the teacher who is best for one child may be less suitable for another. In short, don't jump to conclude that these rumors are accurate. And even when a teacher's performance is not all one hoped it might be, the options opened to a school are not great due to tenure and permanent appointments. This means that in the course of a six-year elementary education, some years may turn out to be better than others.

Let's assume, however, that the reports sound especially true and are not just the more typical unfair rumors. Make an appointment to see the school principal in person and confront him with your concerns. It is almost certain that the principal will back the teacher, revealing at best only some mild criticisms. At that point you can: ask for a change of teacher, appeal the matter to the school superintendent's office, give the teacher the benefit of the doubt, or enroll your child in another school. Most parents are willing to give the teacher a chance. To increase the chances of success, make it a point to meet the teacher at the start of the year to explain your child's background and to establish a good relationship and close communication.

Suppose by October you find your worst fears realized and the teacher does not seem competent. At that point, you can demand a change of teacher. If that fails you should consult with other parents and take the matter to the superintendent or school board. All of these dramatic actions will be painful and should be avoided unless you truly have no faith in the teacher and school principal.

### What are heterogeneous and homogeneous grouping?

Essentially, these are the two ways to form groups. *Homogeneously* means putting together students of roughly the same achievement level and *heterogeneously* means mixing achievement levels. Some people mistakenly think of homogeneous groups as being formed on the basis of ability. This is not true. They're usually formed on the basis of factors such as standardized test scores, grades, and teacher recommendations — all of which look at achievement, not innate ability.

*Tracking* is an extreme version of homogeneous grouping: the formation of whole classes by achievement level. This is very common in middle schools and high schools, and although less common in elementary school, it does exist in some.

Both homogeneous and heterogeneous groups have their place. The typical elementary school reading and math groups, for example, are homogeneous groups. When students are learning new skills that require previous mastery of other skills—as is the case in reading and math—it makes sense to group students who are working at roughly the same level. Otherwise, it doesn't.

### My child often writes his letters and numbers backwards. Could he have dyslexia?

Reversing letters and numbers is extremely common in kindergarten and first grade students. You should put your fears to rest unless it continues into the second grade, but even then an occasional reversal is nothing to be concerned about. You can help your child with his handwriting by reinforcing the papers done correctly with praise, and asking him to look carefully and correct the reversals. But it is not a good idea to make too much fuss over it. As he grows and develops, his handwriting will improve. However, if you feel he is having trouble copying from the chalkboard, check with his teacher to see where he sits in the classroom. A simple move to the front of the class may help the problem.

### Should first graders get homework?

It depends on what *kind* of homework. If your child is expected to complete purple "ditto" sheets night after night, she will quickly tire of this and learn to dread homework despite the fact that she has eleven more years of it to look forward to.

If, on the other hand, your child is given occasional creative assignments, or a small amount of extra work to help her master a skill she is having difficulty with, these would prove appropriate examples of homework for first grade.

Generally speaking, any assignment she is given should not require more than 15 minutes per evening. Much more than that would exceed a first grader's attention span and become miserable for all involved.

You can help your child by establishing a homework routine. Make sure your child has a designated adequate work space for completing homework. It is a good idea to get her in the habit *now* of sitting down in a specific area at a specific time to complete her assignments.

If you are still concerned about her homework assignments, question the teacher concerning her objective for the assignment.

*Why is it that my child can spend 7 hours a day at school, and yet invariably he will answer "nothing", or "I can't remember", when I ask him what he did at school that day?*

"I remember that day at the children's museum!" shouts Fritz, age four. And amazingly, he does remember—detail after detail. But when you ask, "What did you do at school today?" he even has trouble recalling which children he played with! This apparent inconsistency is normal, according to Judith Hudson, Ph.D., a psychologist at Rutgers University.

In her research with three to five year olds, Dr. Hudson found that the children were very accurate in their recall of unusual events, such as the first day of school or a family holiday. But their memories for familiar happenings tend to be weak. "If a situation becomes routine for a child, specific events become blurred," says Hudson.

If you are eager to share a few details about your child's day, try these ideas that may help you get a better conversation going:

- Talk about *your* experiences. If you discuss the events in your day or share how you felt when you started school, your children will be more inclined to do the same.
- Ask specific, informed questions. Learn the names of your child's classmates, then ask about who did what at show and tell, or on the playground. Or ask what stories the teacher read to the class.
- Talk casually about school while you do other things together. Some of the best conversations occur when you and your child are engaged in an absorbing but relaxing activity such as reading or cooking.
- Ask open-ended questions, rather than ones that can be answered

yes or no. In the same way, queries that start with *why* and *which* may lead to more revealing answers.

- Respect your child's need for privacy. Children need some control over when and where they discuss their feelings with you.
- Listen actively; make brief comments that encourage your child to keep talking. And remember: It's easier to draw a child out if you don't pass judgement on what he says.

The Nobel Prize-winning physicist Isidor Isaac Rabi provides an instructive story about his mother's contribution to his intellectual development during his school years: "My mother made me a scientist without ever intending to. Every other Jewish mother in Brooklyn would ask her child after school: 'So? Did you learn anything in school today?' But not my mother. 'Izzy,' she would say, 'did you ask a good *question* today?' That difference—asking good questions—made me become a scientist."

***Our school board is considering year-round schooling. What is the reasoning for this?***

Year-round schooling marks a radical break with the past 300 years of traditional schooling. The nine-month school year is a holdover from the time when even the youngest farmhands were required to plant, cultivate, and harvest the crops. For years, critics have argued that the traditional school year is not only out of date but also is bad education and worse economics.

In 1992, there were more than 2,000 public and private schools in session year-round, representing an increase of about 25 percent from the previous year, so it is definitely a growing trend.

Many education reformers believe that year-round schooling is one way to bring the test scores of American school children up to par with higher scores in Japan and other countries. In traditional schools, children returning from a three-month summer vacation often spend a month or more at the beginning of the new school year reviewing the previous year's material. Some reformers say that with shorter vacations, a child retains more and covers more academic ground. They also contend that the traditional educational system in the U.S. may be contributing to our global economic problems by not adequately preparing American children to compete in the business world.

Sam Sava, Ph.D., who heads the National Association of Elementary School Principals, says "The only nation with a school year shorter than ours is Belgium, with 160 days." Japan's school year is 243 days; Taiwan's,

240; South Korea's and Israel's 220; and Scotland's 200. In a recent survey of elementary school principals, nearly one-third advocated extending our school year—now averaging 175 to 180 days—to 200 days; 38 percent endorsed year-round schooling, with vacations distributed throughout the year. Even though three extra weeks in a school calendar may not sound like much, over 12 years that adds up to a whole *extra year* of education.

Emlyn Griffith, past president of the National Association of State Boards of Education, recommends a school year of up to 240 days, arranged in six 40-day terms. In Griffith's plan, five of the terms would be required, with the sixth offered to students who need remediation or who desire enrichment or special programs such as occupational education, and supplementary language instruction.

However, it is unlikely that there will be widespread adoption of additional, more comprehensive schooling if the money is not available. If teachers are to work more days, their salaries must also be increased. Sava estimates the cost of a longer school year to be an additional $11 billion to $20 billion a year.

***What is the best way to get results when complaining about something I don't like at my son's school?***

- Begin by writing down the *specific* things that are bothering you. This will help you sort out the real concerns from your general feelings of dissatisfaction with the school.
- Try to determine who is most likely to provide some satisfaction. If, for example, you think the teacher doesn't include enough science instruction in the curriculum, consult the *teacher.* If you are unhappy about cafeteria behavior, see the principal or assistant. If your concern is with more than one school or with school policy, see the superintendent. In most school districts elected or appointed school board members are also receptive to complaints, but usually refer them to the staff for investigation.
- If your concern is about the instruction in the school, prepare for your meeting by collecting examples of your child's work.
- If possible, both parents should attend the meeting. This way, you can both raise concerns, hear responses, and sort things out.
- Admit the possibility that there is more than one side to the situation.
- Permit time for improvement. Set a date for a follow-up meeting, by

which point some progress may have been made. If not, then appeal up the chain of command.

- Keep detailed notes on all of your meetings and phone calls.
- Try to arrange your meeting a few days in advance, and be specific about its purpose. Most school personnel will do their homework in advance, given the chance.

# Chapter 13

# PREPARING FOR THE FIRST DAY OF SCHOOL

## TEN POINTS TO DISCUSS WITH YOUR CHILD
## BEFORE THE FIRST DAY

As the first day of school approaches, you will probably prepare for the big event by visiting the school and describing it to your child. You know the important details: where to drop your child off and where to pick her up, what to have her bring and what to have her leave at home.

But *now* is the time to consider how to talk to your child about the first days and weeks of school. The best way to reassure her about this new experience is to let her know what she can expect. You can start by saying, "Let's sit down and talk about what your day is going to be like." It's helpful to find a special time or place to talk: in the car or during a quiet time in the afternoon, when you have your child's attention. You will likely have to repeat much of what you say several times. And don't be surprised if your child has no questions; those will come once school has started.

For the easiest possible transition, child experts suggest these 10 crucial points to discuss with your child:

1. Describe in great detail what the first day of school will be like, beginning with getting dressed and eating breakfast. You can prepare your child for change by giving her a sense of predictability. The child will feel secure in knowing what is going to happen and what will be expected of her.

Speak concretely of some things your child can expect. You can tell her that she will be walking into a big hallway and taking a stairway to the classroom, for example, or you can explain circle time and describe the playground.

2. Explain *beforehand* how you will say good-bye and separate. "I'll give you a kiss and a hug and then I'll be gone." Also, an object from a parent or from home can be very comforting to a child. Give your child

an object of yours, such as a handkerchief. For some reason, children are convinced that you'll come back to get a thing, even more than you'll come back to get *them*. It's an anchor for them.

Another helpful tactic is help your child develop a mental picture of what you will be doing while the two of you are separated. Tell your child something like, "While you're coloring inside or playing on the playground, I'll be working in my office (or at home, cleaning up and getting dinner ready)." This reassures your child to think of you in surroundings that *she* is familiar with. It also helps her to realize that some important things in her life haven't changed.

3. Explain to your child that just as it is your job to help her at home, it's the teacher's job to help her at school. Saying something like, "The teacher is your friend," won't help; your child knows that she is not, yet. However, it *is* helpful to say, "The teacher will take good care of you; she likes children."

4. Explain to your child that some things will be done differently than they are at home, and the teacher has a set of rules that everyone must follow. At home your child doesn't have to raise her hand to talk or line up to walk down a hall. But soon she will be expected to follow a schedule, listen to unfamiliar grown-ups, and share on a regular basis, so you'll want to encourage her to follow the rules and customs of group living.

5. Explain to your child that there is a bathroom at school for her to use, and that all she has to do is tell the teacher when she needs to use it. This may sound unnecessary to you, but many children are actually too shy, or embarrassed to ask about the bathroom on the first day of meeting a new teacher and peers, and may end up having an embarrassing accident.

6. It is important that your child has experienced a few lengthy separations prior to this one. Explain to your child how long the two of you will be separated so that she will not become overly anxious or upset when she realizes half the day is gone and you still aren't there.

7. A good way to reassure your child and explore her fears is to talk about when an older sibling or *you* were beginning school. Explain that feeling nervous is *normal*. Don't try to reassure your child by saying that all the other children will be nervous too. If she walks in her new school and sees children enjoying themselves, she will think you don't understand or don't know what you are talking about.

8. Explain that as time goes by, each day will get a little easier and a little less scary.

9. Tell your child exactly who will pick her up and when. And whatever you do, *don't be late on the first day.* This can be terrifying to a young child who doesn't understand the routine yet.

10. Let your child know that when she gets home from school, you will sit down and talk to her all about what happened. Answer any questions she has, and take them seriously. She will need a little extra time with you now more than ever, because her world has changed forever and she needs some extra security.

Your words of comfort and support will make the transition from home to school smooth and enjoyable. What you tell her holds enormous value and meaning.

About a week or two before kindergarten starts try the following suggestions to help further smooth the transition:

- Drive or walk by the school with your child and look around the playground (the important part to your child).
- If your child is going to take the bus, walk to the bus stop too.
- Take advantage of any opportunities that the school offers ahead of time to take a peek inside or meet the teacher. (Some schools plan a get-together the day before school starts or hold an "open house" during teacher preplanning work days.)
- "School starts a week from Monday." If your child is having a hard time understanding exactly when that is, buy a roll of Life Savers® and tell him "Eat one of these every night, but only one, and when you get to the end of the roll, the next morning will be the first day of school." You, of course, will have to monitor the roll, one a night, but your child will be able to count through the aluminum foil, how many days are left.
- Consider arranging a play date for your child and a neighborhood child or someone else who will be in the same class. It will be reassuring for your child to recognize a friendly face on the first day of school.
- Create September rituals together such as choosing a lunch box, a set of pencils or a new pair of shoes.
- Establish bedtime and wake-up routines and practice getting up and going to bed on the new schedule.
- Read a book together about going to kindergarten (see suggestions

in Chapter 8) and use it as a springboard for discussion about any last-minute concerns.

- Take a cue from your child. If he isn't overly anxious about beginning school, don't get overly excited or emotional in front of him about this rite of passage. If your child senses that you are at all anxious, he will be anxious too.

Of course, your words can't solve every problem or protect your child from every pitfall. Much as you might like to clear the path he takes, you can't prepare him for everything. But that's the way it should be: With your encouragement, your child will learn how to negotiate the challenges of the larger world.

### The Child Who Adjusts Slowly

What if, in spite of your best efforts, you find that your child balks at going to school or resists your leave-takings? Her distress may occur on the way to school, as you say good-bye, or even after three or four days of peaceful separations. A child may tell you that she's scared, dissolve into tears, or be furious in her protests.

You can begin by saying, "This sounds like it's really scary for you" or, "You sound really angry." But block the impulse to make these feelings go away by insisting that school is great, or that all the children are her friends. Then you have really convinced her that you're unaware of how she feels. It's better to ask, "What can we do to make it less scary for you?"

Your child might come up with a real problem that can be addressed — for instance, she may have fallen victim to a bully early on, or she may have interpreted a teacher's request to wait and use the bathroom as meaning that she would have to wait until she went home. Another child might simply want a parent to stay for a while in the classroom for a few days longer. (If you do stay, make sure that you're boring; joining in the fun will only delay the child's realization that school is for *her.*)

If the child can come up with no specific explanation for her fear or anxiety, it's best to drop the subject, then try again later when the child is calm. It might be very helpful to play school at home, using teddy bears or dolls. This is a way to "rehearse" the rituals of the day in advance. You might pick up clues by watching the child's play or by listening to what she says.

If things continue to be difficult at morning drop-off time, you might want to schedule a talk with the head of the school and/or your child's teacher. It's easy to feel embarrassed when your child cries and clings to you while her classmates seem to be marching merrily through the door. But nursery school teachers have seen every variety of behavior, and they are usually prepared with helpful suggestions based on their experience. After you and the staff talk over the situation, the consensus may be that your child is, in fact, ready for the next step. At that point, the staff will probably advise you to tell your youngster you are going to leave, and then do it. If you are convinced that this is the right school for her and that she will be happy there once she gets used to it, you must trust the staff to help your child make her adjustment. Almost always, you will hear from them later that she's become engaged in the class within a few moments of your leaving.

## CHECK-UPS AND IMMUNIZATIONS

When your child enters school, you will be required to show proof that she has been properly immunized. This is a good time to take your child for a check-up and make sure her immunizations are up to date.

In preparation for the doctor's visit, keep in mind that it can be a positive learning experience and that a youngster's responses to a doctor are shaped by their age, temperament and most importantly, by the cues they get from their parents. By preparing your children for regular check-ups and examinations, you can help relieve any anxieties they may have. Start by using simple, clear language. Explain why you are going to the doctor and the main things that will happen. Also, books are a good way to introduce the topic (see Chapter 8 under "Doctor Visits" for a list). Let your child pick out a favorite item to take along with her for comfort. Books or crayons and paper can keep her engaged while you're in the waiting area.

Most states require that all children be immunized against eight diseases: diphtheria, pertussis (whooping cough), tetanus, measles, mumps, rubella (German measles), poliomyelitis, and Haemophilus influenza type B (bacterial meningitis). These vaccinations, typically administered between the ages of two months and 16 years, are generally quite safe. By the age of two, children should have received 80 percent of these immunizations against dangerous illnesses according to the Centers for Disease Control and Prevention (CDC) in Atlanta. However, millions of children are not adequately immunized, despite the fact that these diseases can be quite dangerous.

Be honest with your child about the injections or any other potentially painful procedures. Tell her that it may hurt or pinch for just a second. Explain that the shot is to prevent her from getting a bad disease and that it will only take a second before it is over with. If you tell a four year old "This isn't going to hurt," and it does, the child's faith in you will be shaken. And then whom can your child trust if she ever has to undergo a really painful procedure? After an uncomfortable visit, it is a good idea to reward your child with a favorite treat or activity. Praise her for being brave *before* she has a chance to lose control.

## VISION AND HEARING PROBLEMS

It is also a good idea to have your child's vision and hearing checked. Although schools routinely conduct vision and hearing checks, your child may not be tested until his second or third month of school. Vision and hearing problems are the culprit of many difficulties children experience in school. The sooner a problem is diagnosed, the sooner it can be corrected.

### Common Vision Problems

When Emily, age four, is playing outside, she always sees the far end of the street as a blur of color. Her friend Christopher can see the far end of the street just fine, but when he looks at a book, the letters are fuzzy. Both of these children have a vision disorder, but—like most children with such problems—they think everyone sees things the same way they do.

While preschool eye tests provide some information about a child's eyesight, parents are really the best detectors of preschool children's vision problems, according to the American Optometric Association.

Common difficulties include nearsightedness, farsightedness, color vision deficiencies, and visual-perception problems. Your child may have a problem if he consistently:

- Sits too close to the television, prefers reading or other close work to sports and outdoor games, and squints or is tense when looking at an object in the distance.
- Prefers sports and outdoor games to reading or other close work, and squints or is tense when looking at close objects.

- Has difficulty seeing a difference between shades of red and green, or blue and yellow.
- Rubs his eyes, daydreams, or becomes restless and irritable when doing close work, and is less skilled than other kids his age in climbing stairs or throwing and catching a ball.

A child with an undetected vision problem may be incorrectly diagnosed as having a learning disability. Vision problems can usually be treated with corrective lenses or exercises prescribed by an optometrist or ophthalmologist.

### Common Hearing Problems

Three million children in the United States have some degree of hearing impairment. Because learning to speak centers on the imitation of perceived sound, young children who are hard of hearing have a double handicap.

If your child experienced chronic ear infections as an infant and or toddler, there is a chance that his hearing was affected. This hearing loss makes it difficult for children to distinguish between similar sounds, such as man and fan or cap and can. In many cases where a child is suspected of having speech problems, the *cause* of the speech problem is found to be a slight hearing loss. The affected child does not hear the complete sound of a word. For example, he may pronounce the word bird as "urd." Fortunately, the majority of these children can improve the quality of both their hearing and their speech with hearing aids, speech therapy, and auditory training. So if you suspect a problem, see your pediatrician immediately.

Even if hearing seems to be developing normally, your doctor should check your child's ears two or three times during the first year, and twice during the second and third years. Being aware of your child's response to sound from birth will help you determine if your child is hard of hearing. Here is a list of the danger signals:

- Birth to three months: is not startled by sharp clap within three to six feet; is not soothed by mother's voice.
- Three to six months: does not turn eyes or head to search for source of sound; does not imitate his own noises; does not enjoy sound making toys, such as rattles.
- Six to ten months: does not respond to own name, a ringing telephone,

or a voice at speaking level; does not respond to common words such as "bye-bye."

- Ten to fifteen months: cannot point to or look at familiar objects or people when asked to; does not imitate simple words and sounds.
- Fifteen to eighteen months: cannot follow simple spoken directions like "pick it up" or "give it to Mommy"; is not beginning to build a simple vocabulary.
- All ages: is not awakened or disturbed by loud sounds; does not respond when called; pays no attention to ordinary noises, uses gestures, not words to communicate needs; watches parent's face intently.

For more information on vision and hearing problems, see the associations listed in the appendix at the end of this book.

Contact your local health department for a vision and hearing screening for your child. Most health departments provide this service for free or for a very small fee.

## GETTING ORGANIZED

### The Morning Routine

The problem with the morning routine is that parents and children have conflicting agendas. The child wants to wake up and play; and the parent wants to wake up and get to work. The following is a list of tips to help your morning routine run more smoothly:

- Be sure to keep morning activities structured, because children are often not as aware of the passing of time and can take on too many things at once and get side tracked easily, no matter how well meaning.
- Break down the morning goals into time frames and prioritize them. Ten to 15 minute segments for each task work best. Also, work around personalities. Slow to wake children often prefer to get in gear over breakfast and once they're refueled they can proceed to getting dressed, etc.
- Working backward from your estimated time of departure, outline a schedule for each family member and (this is the hard part) put it into practice.
- Make sure that your children are rising early enough so that they

don't spend their entire morning in a frantic rush, allow for them to take their time and have a pleasant morning.

- Never send your child to school without breakfast because "there wasn't time." Your child will not be able to do his best at school the day you send him without eating.
- Reschedule as much of the morning routine as possible for the night before.
  - Lay out tomorrow's outfit
  - Locate shoes and jacket
  - Put lunch money or important notes or papers in envelope labeled with child's name and teacher
  - Stuff bookbag or backpack with all necessary materials and place by the door
  - Prepare lunches the night before
  - Set the breakfast table with nonperishables (cereal boxes, etc.)
  - Take five minutes to locate the items *you* tend to search for in the morning (keys, glasses, etc.)
- Prepare for the next day's weather gear by taking a peek at the weather forecast for tomorrow. Dress your child in layers on days when the morning is very cool and the afternoon is much warmer.
- Post a chalk or bulletin board where you will see it upon leaving your house. Leave reminders concerning what is needed and when. Post a pocket under the board and train your children to leave notes, permission slips and important papers in the pocket. (Make sure that the pocket is low or small enough that papers are visible.)
- Post a family calendar on or near the family board, detailing school and family activities and events.
- Keep the children's library books on one shelf or table in the house. After they read them, make sure they put them back on the shelf. That way you won't have to search through the books in their room looking for the borrowed ones.
- If you are aware of what your child is learning in school, briefly discuss with him the day's lesson. (Some schools even send a calendar home at the first of each month detailing the month's lessons and activities.)
- Establish a file for your child's important papers. Keep them all together in a safe place.
- Give each child his own alarm clock so he can get himself up in the morning.

- If adequate bathroom time is a problem in your family, stock your children's rooms with mirrors, hair dryers (for older children), clothes hampers, hooks and towel racks, anything that can be done in the bedroom instead of the bathroom.
- No parent can do it all. As early as possible, teach children to pitch in.

If your children are in the habit of parking themselves in front of the television before breakfast, insist that no one watch TV until he is dressed and his lunch box and backpack are ready to go.

According to Edward Christophersen, Ph.D., a pediatric psychologist in Kansas City, Missouri, and author of *Beyond Discipline: Parenting That Lasts a Lifetime,* "Little people should be taught to live by the same rules, scaled down, that big people live by." This he emphasizes, gives children the resources they'll need as adults.

A parent's job is to help their children help themselves. Then when they can go it alone, phase yourself out.

## RIDING THE SCHOOL BUS

Nearly 25 million children ride the school bus each year. Sadly, each year an average of 38 children are killed while trying to board or exit a bus. Of those killed, half are 5 or 6 year olds. Had they been taught the rules for school bus safety, more carefully by their bus drivers *and* their parents, many of those deaths could have been prevented. Data on school bus accidents show that children are at a greater risk of being killed as pedestrians in a school bus *loading zone* than as passengers on a school bus. A typical fatality occurs when a child drops something after exiting a bus and dashes back to pick it up after the driver has started the vehicle.

Parents should not rely on the school and the bus driver to teach school bus safety, here are some rules that you should teach your child before he rides the school bus.

1. Be on time.
2. Never run to or from the bus.
3. Stay on the sidewalk while waiting for the bus, not the curb or the street.
4. Check traffic both ways before crossing the street or wait for the driver's signal.

5. Wait for the bus to come to a complete stop.
6. Always cross at least 10 feet in front of the bus, so the driver can always see you.
7. *No matter what you drop, don't run back to retrieve it until the bus and all other traffic has cleared the road.*
8. Never crawl under a school bus.
9. Go directly to a seat and stay there.
10. Do not yell or shout. Don't push or shove.
11. Obey the driver at all times.
12. At railroad crossings, refrain from talking so that the driver may check the crossing properly.

These may seem like common-sense rules and you may incorrectly assume that your child does not require any further instruction than that from his bus driver. But school bus safety is everybody's business and you would be hard pressed to find a school bus driver who would not agree that these rules should be taught at home in addition to school.

If you decide to let your child ride the bus to school, experts agree, it is best to let him ride the first day of school, rather than driving him in the car for the first few days and *then* putting him on the bus. He will make the transition much easier if he is on the bus from the start of the school year. (If you are nervous about this, you can discreetly follow his bus with your car.) Another factor to consider is that if your child rides with you in the car the first week, and *then* you put him on the bus the second week, he has missed the crucial time when the bus driver and school personnel take the time to go over the safety rules carefully and thoroughly. A final hint: take the time to get to know the driver of the bus. After all, this person is in charge of your child every time he gets on the bus. Also, this may prove helpful later on in the year if any small problems arise.

The National Safety Council suggest that parents work with schools to make sure school bus stops and drivers are evaluated for safety. Familiarize yourself with your particular school district's transportation policies. If you have questions or concerns, call the transportation supervisor in your district. If he or she can't or won't address your concerns, take them to the superintendent. If you still don't get results, go to the school board.

# Chapter 14

# WARNING SIGNS OF PROBLEMS

Unfortunately, a child's problem in school does not always present itself in a clear dramatic way. Sometimes we know something isn't quite right, but we can't exactly put our finger on the problem.

It may seem as though a child is not quite performing up to his potential, or perhaps the child is not doing quite as well as we think he should be doing. He may become easily distracted or give up too easily. Perhaps he seems disinterested in everything around him. He may be tired too often, or cranky and irritable all of the time.

Both parents and teachers become frustrated because they feel the child is not working up to his capabilities. But before you start pushing and nagging your child, take a closer look at the situation.

Start by talking with your child. This gives the best clues. Ask your child to "tell you the story of his days." What you should listen for are stories or offhand remarks that suggest something is not quite right.

In the whirlwind of your day-to-day routine, chances are you don't get many opportunities to discover the person your child is becoming. Asking some open-ended questions will help you get to know your child better. Here are some starters:

• Look at what your child enjoys doing and feels competent at, especially the attention, care, and standards to which he holds himself in that activity. Ask him what he does well. How does that compare to his schoolwork?

• Listen to what your child says about himself in comparison with other children in the class. Does he feel competent compared with most of them? Does he believe he is in the right reading group, for example. How satisfied is he with his progress?

• Ask your child what he thinks: Does he believe he is doing his best? In what areas does he think he could improve? How does he think you could help him? What is something he likes about himself?

• Ask your child:

What is the best thing that ever happened to you?
What was the worst?
When you make a mistake, how do you feel?
If you could trade places with anyone in the world, who would it be?
If you could change anything about yourself, what would it be?
If you had three wishes, what would you wish for?

All of these questions can provide valuable and surprising insights into the mind of your child.

Second, review reports from teachers, report cards, tests sent home for signing, etc. Take the time to talk with the child's teacher and or caretaker. Oftentimes these people spend more time with the child during the week than do the parents. Their insights and observations concerning the child could prove to be very helpful, they are often able to make unbiased observations that the parent is unable to see.

This issue is not easily resolved. We don't want to create either overachievers or underachievers. As parents, we must demand that our children do their best and hold high standards for themselves, but we must not pressure them so much that we take the fun out of learning. Pushing children to *always* be the best will ultimately be counterproductive. But we don't want to ignore what looks like persistent underachievement, either. If that is really what is going on, then the next step is to figure out *why* in order to do something about it.

## A CHECKLIST FOR WARNING SIGNS

There are some clear warning signs of problems. Here they are separated into a child's physical, social, emotional, and academic or cognitive growth or development. This is an artificial separation, however, since these areas of growth are all interrelated.

Unfortunately, schools do not always recognize *all* parts of a child's development. They are concerned primarily with a child's academic progress. As parents, it is our responsibility to be particularly aware of the other areas of growth and development.

Please consider these lists from *School Savvy* (Noonday, 1993) by Diane Harrington and Laurette Young, as very rough guides and not exact rules of child development. Use your observation powers and some of the following questions to see if you need to take a closer look.

## Physical Development

- Does your child complain frequently about going to school?
- Are stomach cramps and a sore throat a typical part of the morning routine?
- Does your child find it hard to sit still? At home does he wiggle around all of the time? Is his "motor going" constantly? Does the teacher tell you the same story?
- Does your child often appear tired? Does he have trouble going to sleep at night?
- Do you see a change in your child's eating habits or appetite? Is he suddenly eating a lot less or a lot more? Is he suddenly not interested or very interested in food?
- Does your child seem to have difficulty with fine motor skills (holding and writing with a pencil, for example)? Or with gross motor skills (running, riding a bicycle, and so on)?

## Social Development

- Does your child complain about being lonely?
- Does he have any friends in his class at school or the neighborhood?
- If he doesn't, does he say or act as though it bothers him? Does he talk about it? Does he tell you why he has no friends?
- If he has friends, does he fight with them a lot? Does the teacher tell you the same thing happens in school?
- Does he talk too much in school, and get in trouble for it? What does he say is the reason he talks too much?
- How does your child interact with siblings? With other family members?

## Emotional Development

- Does your child seem anxious or depressed about school or his life in general? (Depression in children can manifest itself in many ways, perhaps a sad face all the time, poor appetite, frequent crying or sighing, or withdrawal.)
- Has your child suddenly become argumentative or rude with his family and in school too?

• Is he nonresponsive to questions about school? Or does he become emotional or upset when school is mentioned?

• Does your child seem to be overly dependent on you? Does he have difficulty separating from you?

• Does your child approach new situations with a great deal of fear or anxiety? Is he so afraid that he won't try new experiences?

## Academic or Cognitive Development

• Have you noticed a sudden drop in your child's grades in one or more subject matters?

• Are the grades lower than what you believe they should be?

• Does your child have persistent difficulty in one area so that he is falling behind his classmates?

• What is your child's attitude about schoolwork? Does he appear overwhelmed by it? Anxious? Unmotivated? Does he give up without even trying when the work is difficult for him?

• Does your child seem very disorganized? Does he leave books and materials in school or at home? Does he lose things often? Is he confused about what is expected of him?

It would be great if I could say to you, "If you answered yes to three or more questions, here's what you do...." Unfortunately, it is not that easy. If you answered yes to some of these questions, it could mean a number of things. To find the answer, this is where the need for more detective work and for *communication* with the school becomes important. This cannot be emphasized enough. Teachers, principals, counselors, and school support staff have a great deal of experience. Children are their business and they have seen hundreds of them in their careers. Their opinions and insights can often prove invaluable as you seek an answer to your child's problem. Talk with them and listen to what they have to say concerning your child.

Some common causes of problems are difficulties or tension in the home environment, scheduling too many activities for the child, immaturity, and fatigue or headaches due to skipping breakfast. Skipping breakfast is not a healthy habit, and it deprives children of the energy that they need to learn. Studies have shown that children who do not eat breakfast perform below par in the classroom because they are not alert and have difficulty concentrating.

It could also be that your child is experiencing problems at school because he is not being challenged enough or because of a mismatch between the child's learning style and the school's.

## SPECIAL PROBLEMS OF CHILDHOOD

A child's behavior is a symptom of a psychological disorder if it:

1. Differs widely from normal behavior
2. Has undesirable consequences or side effects
3. Distresses the child

All three conditions must be present before behavior becomes a symptom of a psychological disorder. For example, a child who shows exceptional ability in school differs greatly from most other school children. But the child's behavior is not considered a symptom because it does not usually have undesirable consequences or cause distress to the child.

A number of childhood problems may be symptoms of deeper physical or psychological disorders. Two of the most common such problems are unrealistic fears and aggressive and antisocial behavior.

### Unrealistic Fears

All children are afraid on occasion. Fear is thus a normal emotion. Fears are unrealistic if they occur regularly in the absence of real danger. In some cases, such fears may be directly related to a frightening past experience. For example, a child who has a fear of all animals may have developed the fear after being attacked by an animal. In other cases, unrealistic fears may be only indirectly related to a past event. For instance, a child who feels extreme guilt over an action may expect severe punishment. The child may then develop an abnormal fear of death, accidents, or illness.

### Aggressive and Antisocial Behavior

Psychologists define aggression as angry, hostile behavior that is intended to hurt or upset others. Such behavior in young children can result from *frustration*. Children may feel frustrated if their demands are not met or if their feelings of worthiness and self-respect are threatened. If the anger is intense, it may erupt into a tantrum—a common form of aggression in young children.

Children can learn to control aggression if they are taught at an early age that some of their demands will not be met. A child who develops *frustration tolerance* is less likely to have severe or frequent tantrums. But children may have great difficulty developing the necessary tolerance if their parents are overly strict or overly permissive. If parents are too strict, a child may feel increasingly frustrated in trying to meet their high goals and standards. If they are too permissive, the child may act aggressively to any frustration. Parents also encourage aggression if they are often angry and hostile themselves.

Most children learn to control aggression by the preteen-age years. They may do so partly by channelling their energies into hobbies, sports, schoolwork, and other activities. Some children, however, do not learn to deal with aggression effectively. Instead these children may relieve feelings of frustration and hostility by antisocial behavior, such as bullying other children, or stealing or destroying property. Such forms of antisocial behavior worsen if the peer group encourages them.

Other special problems may be symptoms of psychological or physical disorders. These problems include:

- hyperactivity (extreme restlessness)
- poor performance in school
- extreme shyness
- divorce
- bedwetting

## Hyperactivity

Most hyperactive children cannot concentrate on anything for more than a few minutes at a time. Scientists do not know the exact cause of the disturbance. There is evidence that some cases may be caused by an allergy to certain chemical additives in food, especially particular food colorings and dyes.

Many teachers have found that some of their hyperactive students' behavior improved dramatically after changing their breakfast and encouraging a set bedtime. A six year old whose bedtime fluctuates from night to night and eats a chocolate breakfast bar with a doughnut washed down with a glass of chocolate milk for breakfast each morning is not as likely to do as well as the child who is in bed promptly at 8:30 every night, and eats fresh fruit and a low sugar cereal for breakfast.

If you're concerned that your child may be hyperactive, there is a simple test you can do at home: Observe his television-watching habits. If he can concentrate for an hour of cartoons or other children's programming, then he most likely isn't hyperactive.

Some hyperactive childrens' behavior is controlled with medication; however, this is not the solution for all children. Visit your doctor and consider making other changes such as schedule consistencies and diet alterations before you resort to any medication. If you do decide that medication is the answer for your child, monitor him carefully and discuss any side effects at length with your physician.

## Poor Performance in School

Poor performance in school is frequently caused by a child's failure to learn to read. Failure in reading may be due to a physical or psychological problem such as poor eyesight, poor hearing, or extreme shyness. The reading ability of most hyperactive or mentally retarded children is severely limited. In many cases, however, reading problems can be avoided if parents prepare their children for learning to read. Parents should thus make a practice of reading stories and poems to their children during the toddler and preschool years. Parents should also acquaint their children with books and other reading materials and help them build a vocabulary. Schoolchildren who lack such preparation may fall behind their classmates in learning to read. Children also need a motive for learning to read. Parents help provide such a motive if they show that they value learning.

## Extreme Shyness

In some cases children become overly shy if they are dominated by older brothers and sisters. Shyness may also begin as an inherited tendency. But the exact causes are not well understood.

Certainly you may help your child overcome his shyness to an extent if you build up his self-esteem. Let him know how much you value him and love him. Intervene when older siblings tease or dominate a shy child. Help him learn to have simple conversations with others by talking with him everyday about whatever might be on his mind.

## Divorce

Although the stress of a divorce for a child is not necessarily greater than the stress of living in a home in which the parents are incompatible and constantly quarreling, a divorce cannot help but be upsetting to a child. The impact of a divorce depends on the relationship of the children to both parents afterward. It takes about two years for children to make the adjustment. During this time a child's otherwise adequate schoolwork may begin to regress. A recently divorced parent should not add to the child's misery by scolding him for inadequate schoolwork. Watch the child for signs and cues of any problems he may have adjusting to this new situation. Many children have an inward tendency to blame themselves for their parents' breakup, even though they may be told otherwise. Or, a child may think, "If Daddy left, Mama might go away one day too!"

Many divorced parents remarry within a few years of the divorce. Generally, remarriage facilitates the resolution of the problem, but it creates problems of its own in the need to adapt to step-parents.

It is important that the child's teacher be aware of what is happening at home. Working patiently, together with the teacher, the child's schoolwork should return to normal within a reasonable amount of time.

## Bedwetting

A habit of bedwetting after about five years of age is a physical or psychological symptom. Parents *should not punish or threaten a child who has this problem!* In *every case* a physician or psychologist should be consulted.

# Chapter 15

# AFTER SCHOOL . . . NOW WHAT?

## AFTER SCHOOL ACTIVITIES

After school activities can be great for an energetic child, but an overload of after school activities may have long-term effects. According to Richard Oberfield, M.D., clinical associate professor of psychiatry at New York University's Medical Center in New York City, children deprived of play time, including time to make up games and pretend, may suffer from a lack of creativity later in life.

In addition to the stress of too much structured time, notes Oberfield, the children are often not interested in the activities. This happens when parents force their own unfulfilled dreams—such as taking up a musical instrument or becoming a great dancer or athlete—on children who have different interest and needs.

But children given ample free time, Oberfield observes, are more likely to develop genuine interests and to pursue them eagerly.

Oberfield urges parents not to sign kids up for activities just because everyone else is doing so. Instead, parents should be sensitive to what their children's needs and interests really are. And *after school activities should be balanced with time to do absolutely nothing.* Most important, parents and children should also spend time together in an unstructured environment. Giving children the feeling of being cared about for themselves, not just for their performance, is integral to their self-esteem.

## HOME ALONE

If you are one of the millions of working parents with young school-age children, you face a tough dilemma—what to do with the children between the time they get out of school, and you get home from work. Many have debated on what age a child is old enough to stay home alone until his parents return from work. Child experts vary on their opinions of this topic, but basically, it boils down to the characteristics and maturity of each individual child. Some children can handle staying home alone for an hour or more at age 7, and others are not ready for this until 12! If you choose to leave your child alone after school, you should *train him* for the following situations:

What to do in case:

- of emergency (define "emergency" for your child)
- of fire
- a stranger comes to the door (define "stranger" for your child)
- someone calls for you
- a prank phone call is received
- the electricity goes out
- you do not come home on time
- they get sick, or scared
- they can't reach you at work
- an accident occurs

A child who stays home alone should know the following information:

- their home address
- their home phone number
- their parents' full names
- how to reach you at work
- whom to call in the event they cannot reach you at work
- how to reach fire and police departments (or 911 in some areas)

Staying home alone is not as much fun as it sounds for most kids. That's what a recent survey by the Camp Fire Boys and Girls has found. Nearly half of the 13 to 18 year olds questioned said they didn't like going home to an empty house when they were 12 or younger. While most of the children said that they learned how to be responsible, half believed that being home alone created stress. Two-thirds of the children — more than 20 percent of them from the time they were 10 or younger — have been left in charge of other kids. And 81 percent of them had not taken a baby-sitting course which would have prepared them for emergencies. More than half of these children had encountered a situation where a stranger came to the door and or a prank phone call was received.

The good news is that more before and after school programs are now available. A recent federal study found that some 1.7 million children —

most of them third-graders or younger—are enrolled in nearly 50,000 programs.

## CHOOSING THE RIGHT DAY CARE
## OR PRESCHOOL PROGRAM FOR YOUR CHILD

As you begin to investigate the various child care programs available in your area you may wonder to what extent the labels "nursery school," "day care center," "prekindergarten," and "child development center" and so on reflect actual differences in program quality and goals.

Program quality varies sometimes greatly from center to center and the traditional differences among all four kinds of settings have become very blurred. However, the following capsule descriptions may help you to focus your search:

**Nursery School.** This is the traditional early-childhood model and is typically operated on a tuition basis during regular school hours. Parents often may choose a morning or afternoon session. Many established schools are of high quality, but the short hours can be a problem for those who need child care. Many are lengthening hours or offering child-care options.

**Day-Care Center.** These centers are based on the custodial needs of families for out-of-home care of young children. Many are open from 6:00 or 7:00 A.M. until 6:00 or 7:00 P.M. Many are publicly financed. Good centers have a child-development and educational focus rather than *just* custodial care. High quality day-care centers provide comprehensive child services including health care.

**Child-Development Center.** Sometimes these programs are operated in conjunction with universities, hospitals, or school systems. Some are designed for children with special needs. Some have specific philosophies or goals. Nearly all child-development centers have parent education components, and some also involve home-based activities. If university or hospital affiliated, they may have research and diagnostic components.

**Prekindergarten Programs.** These programs, designed primarily for four year olds, go by a variety of names, including "early childhood centers." If they are tied to the local school system, they are often located in a school building and are usually free. Typically they focus on introducing children to and readying them for the regular school experience. In some states, such as California, there is a movement toward full integration of these programs into the public schools.

As you look into the available choices you will find considerable overlap in functions and wide variations in sponsorship and cost. The bottom line questions should be, Which program best fits the needs of our family? and Which program seems most sensitive to the developmental needs of my child?

Many parents end up choosing a center solely on the basis of what's convenient or what a friend has recommended. Although there are plenty of good programs, finding the *right* one usually means throwing away preconceptions and looking to the person who can best guide parents—their own child.

It's now easier for parents to translate their hunches into a more objective understanding of their child, thanks to the work of child development experts such as Dr. Stella Chess, a professor of child psychiatry at New York University Medical Center. Chess and a colleague, Dr. Alexander Thomas, initiated a project in 1956 to follow 133 infants into adulthood. Their report, the *New York Longitudinal Study,* coauthored with Herbert Birch, defines a number of important personality traits in children. Using their categories as a guide, parents can now assess a child's strengths and needs—and make those hard-to-put-into-words qualities more concrete.

**Activity Level.** Everyone knows at least one child who seems to be a bundle of energy, constantly running from one activity to the next. Parents of such children should take this energy level into account when they look at programs. If you have a very rambunctious child, and the program doesn't give him enough opportunity to run around, look elsewhere. Conversely, shy children often do better in settings with smaller groups.

**Predictability.** Some children sleep, wake up, and eat at the same time each day; others go to sleep at 7:30 one night and 10:00 the next. Most programs, particularly larger more institutional programs, follow a daily schedule that children who need regularity will find comforting. However, if a child has trouble adjusting to say a naptime schedule—if he simply isn't sleepy—then it's best for him to have a teacher who is flexible enough to let him do some quiet activity while the others are sleeping.

**Adaptability.** There are children who can bound into a new setting and adjust easily, joining the reading time or art project or whatever is going on. For children who hold back, it's important to find a program where the teachers make an effort to involve them.

**Sensory Threshold.** Although there are many young children who thrive in a busy program, other children have a lower tolerance for noise and commotion, and become easily overwhelmed by a raucous playroom. Some programs have *too* many choices for kids making them a very busy place. Your child may prefer a classroom that had some relatively private areas, like a reading corner, so that she could retreat for some time to herself.

Noise and activity aren't the only things that can overstimulate children— even too many bright colors may be tough on them. Adults may go into a visually busy room and say, "Oh, what wonderful colors!" But for a child, lots of toys and things on the walls can be overwhelming.

**Attention Span.** A child who will only play with a new toy for a few minutes or who loses interest in drawing after the first try should be in a program where the teacher makes sure she learns some follow-through.

**Liberty and Limits.** Some schools let children choose between outdoor play areas and indoor art and dress-up activities. There are children who flourish in this kind of atmosphere. Other schools operate with an abundance of rules about where to sit, when to speak, when to play outside, etc. These can be a good setting for children who need more limits.

Parents can more easily navigate the universe of preschools and child care programs once they have a good understanding of their child's personality. To simplify this search, parents should forget about educational buzzwords and focus on the teachers, teaching style or caregivers. To find the right program start by visiting schools. Try to find a child who is like your own and watch how the teacher interacts with him in a group situation.

## A Word About The Preschool Environment

In search of stimulating environments for their children, many parents choose "academic" programs in which the day is organized into classes covering math, reading, and even foreign language and computers. Although preschools are learning places—or at least they should be—many early childhood experts caution against a high pressure curriculum, no matter what the temperament of the child. "I don't think there is any place for that in a preschool," says Nancy Close, a lecturer in psychology at Yale University and its Child Study Center. "Developmentally, preschoolers aren't ready for formal reading and math lessons; they may become anxious or bored."

To avoid this kind of pressure, parents should look for a school where teachers encourage young children to learn about the world in concrete ways, rather than by memorizing passively. When a child is playing in a block corner, she'll see that the blocks come in different sizes—some twice the size of others, others three times as big. A good teacher might say, "This building keeps falling down; why do you think that is?" And without any mention of math, the child will learn about ratios and estimating.

## Finding the Best Care: A Checklist

In any childcare situation, you should always find out as much as you can before making a decision. Here are some questions you can ask to get a feel for a program's depth of understanding of its mission:

1. Does the primary caregiver have a solid professional background, and is she linked with professional childcare organizations?

2. Did this person have, as a part of her course work, specific training in toddler and or preschool care?

3. Is staff participation in training ongoing?

4. Does the program have a statement of philosophy? If so, ask for a copy.

5. Is individualization emphasized? Check the daily schedule. If it is structured so that all children are supposed to be doing the same things—looking at books or taking a nap—watch out.

6. Will the program give you the names of several parents whose children are currently enrolled, as well as several who are no longer using its services? If so, talk to these parents about the program.

7. Are you expected to participate in the program? What are your responsibilities and rights?

8. What are the program's policies regarding payment, and sick care?

## A Day-Care Safety Checklist

To ensure that your child-care arrangements are safe, the National SAFE KIDS Campaign in Washington, D.C., recommends that all parents conduct a safety review of their day-care center, family day-care home, or preschool. Here is a checklist to help:

1. Does the provider have a certificate of training in pediatric CPR

and basic first aid from the Red Cross, American Heart Association, or any other qualified organization?

2. Does the provider conduct periodic fire drills, and are there smoke detectors and fire extinguishers mounted in each room?

3. Are emergency numbers posted for easy reference?

4. Are parents given written guidelines on what will be done if their child becomes sick or injured while in day care? Likewise, are parents instructed on when sick children should *not* be brought to day care?

5. Is there a strict policy on whom will be allowed to pick up your child?

6. Are electric outlets covered, and high and low cabinets securely locked?

7. Are poisonous houseplants kept out of reach?

8. Are stairwells closed off from children, yet easily accessible for emergency evacuation?

9. Do the children and staff wash their hands before handling food, after using the bathroom, and after changing a diaper?

10. Are toys sterilized frequently? Washable toys should be laundered, and other toy surfaces should be cleaned with diluted household bleach.

11. Are toys safe and age appropriate and kept on open shelves instead of toy chests which can close on children's heads or fingers?

12. Are cleaning products stored in high, locked cabinets and is the phone number for the Poison Control Center posted for easy access? (800-282-5846)

13. Is the environment free of small objects that could be swallowed?

14. Is the diaper changing area located far away from the food area?

15. Is outside play equipment free of sharp edges, rust, cracks, and splinters? Are surfaces under slides and swings soft?

16. Is the amount of floor space adequate for the number of children and are there an adequate number of supervising adults in charge at all times?

17. Are swimming pools, decorative fountains, or ponds fenced off or securely covered?

18. Are certified car seats used on trips away from the home or center?

## The First Days At Day-Care

Start talking about day care a week or so before the big day. Give your child examples of who will be there (adults and children), what she will find (toys and books), and what she will do (play outside, take a nap). Then visit the center with your child and point out everything that you've been telling her about.

Supply your child with visual props to help bring future events into the present. Crossing off the days on the calendar and reading her a book about day-care will help make the idea real to your child. For additional suggestions, try the books *Betsy's First Day at Day Care,* by Gunilla Wolde (Random House), and *Will You Come Back For Me?* by Ann Tompert (Albert Whitman & Company).

Allow your child to bring along a transitional object, such as her favorite blanket or a teddy bear. Remain positive even if you are experiencing a range of emotions. If your child senses that you are at all anxious, she will be anxious too.

# A FINAL NOTE

Once your child starts school, your work does not end there. *You* are the one ultimately responsible for ensuring that your child's education is adequate. You can do so by:

- Keeping informed of what's going on in your child's school. Be involved.
- Keep in constant contact with your child's teacher. Attend all teacher conferences.
- Review *all* papers your child brings home from school. Sit down and go over them together. Encourage your child to tell you about each assignment. Look for areas he does well in and praise him. Help him correct and review the skills he seems to have trouble with.
- Do not hesitate to question the school or the teacher if you have questions concerning the curriculum or the quality of your child's education.
- Show your child that you are *interested and concerned* about what and how he is doing at school. Talk with him often about what is going on and *listen,* without making comments that might subconsciously discourage him from opening up and talking frankly.
- Help your child develop a love and respect for learning and his school and teachers, by showing that respect yourself.
- Be observant and examine any seemingly troubling areas *before* they get out of hand.
- Take the time to know your child's friends. Are they appropriate playmates with similar values?
- Set routines and schedules for meals, homework, play, and TV.
- And most important, love your child *unconditionally,* just the way he is.

# APPENDICES

# APPENDIX A

# NATIONAL ORGANIZATIONS

The following organizations offer publications which give advice to parents or lists other resources. Most of the publications are free, however some do charge a nominal fee. Many of these act as advocacy organizations on behalf of parents and children.

**Academy for Educational Development**
100 Fifth Avenue
New York, NY 10011
212-243-1110

**Alexander Graham Bell Association for the Deaf, Inc.**
3417 Volta Place NW
Washington D.C. 20007
202-337-5220

**American Association of School Administrators**
1801 North Moore Street
Arlington, VA 22209
703-528-0700

**American Montessori Society**
150 Fifth Avenue
New York, New York 10011

**American Federation of Teachers**
555 New Jersey Avenue. NW
Washington, D.C.
202-879-4400

**Association for Childhood Education International**
11501 Georgia Avenue, Suite 315
Wheaton, MD 20902
301-942-2443

**Association for Children and Adults with Learning Disabilities (ACLD)**
4156 Library Road
Pittsburgh, PA 15234
Send $1 postpaid to receive a packet of information, including a bibliography of the ACLD's 800 plus publications and brochures concerning IEP's and parents' rights.

**Association for the Gifted Council on Exceptional Children**
1920 Association Drive
Reston, VA 22091-1589
703-620-3660

**Center for Media Education**
P.O. Box 33039
Washington, D.C. 20033-0039

**Childcare Registry**
P.O. Box 1027
Union City, CA 94587-1027
800-CCR-0033
Founded in 1992, The ChildCare Registry is the first comprehensive service dedicated to the background information verification and registration of child care providers nationwide.

**Children's Defense Fund**
122 C Street, N.W., Suite 400
Washington, DC 20001
202-628-8787

**Educational Equity Concepts, Inc.**
114 East 32nd Street
New York, NY 10016
212-725-1803

**Educational Reference and Information Center Clearinghouse on Disability and Gifted Education**
Council for Exceptional Children
1920 Association Drive
Reston, Virginia 22091-1589
800-328-0272

**Educational Reference and Information Center Clearinghouse on Elementary and Early Childhood Education**
University of Illinois
805 W. Pennsylvania Avenue
Urbana, Illinois 61801
800-583-4135
Write for a publications list which includes short articles on various topics of interest to parents and teachers, free of charge.

**Educational Reference and Information Center Clearinghouse on Reading, English, and Communication**
Indiana University
Smith Research Center, Suite 150
2805 E. 10th Street
Bloomington, Indiana 47408-2698

**Family Math Program, Equals Program**
Lawrence Hall of Science
University of California
Berkeley, CA 94720
510-642-1823

**Family Science Program, Northwest Equals**
Portland State University
Portland, OR 97207
800-547-8887, ext. 3045

**Federation for Children with Special Needs**
95 Berkeley Street, Suite 104
Boston, MA 02116
617-482-2915

**Institute for Responsive Education**
605 Commonwealth Avenue
Boston, MA 02215
617-353-3309

**International Reading Association**
800 Barksdale Road
P.O. Box 8139
Newark, DE 19714
800-336-READ

**Learning Disability Association of America**
4156 Library Road
Pittsburgh, PA 15234
412-341-1515

**National Association for the Education of Young Children**
1509 16th Street, N.W.
Washington, D.C. 20036
800-424-2460

**National Association for Family Day-Care**
815 15th Street, N.W., Suite 928
Washington, D.C. 20005
202-347-3356

**National Center for Fair and Open Testing (Fairtest)**
342 Broadway
Cambridge, MA 02139
617-864-4810

**National Coalition for Parent Involvement in Education National Community Education Association**
801 North Fairfax Street, Suite 209
Alexandria, VA 22314
703-359-8973

**National Center for Learning Disabilities, Inc. (NCLD)**
99 Park Avenue, 6th Floor
New York, NY 10016
NCLD has two publications of interest to parents. *Their World* is a magazine that presents real life stories of how families cope with learning-disabled children. Send a check or money order for $5. In addition, NCLD publishes a comprehensive resource guide, a state-by-state directory of special programs, schools and services for those with learning disabilities. Send $12 for a copy.

**National Coalition of Advocates for Students**
100 Boylston Street, Suite 737
Boston, MA 02116
617-357-8507

**National Congress of Parents and Teachers (PTA)**
700 North Rush Street
Chicago, IL 60611
312-787-0977
and
2000 L Street, N.W., Suite 600
Washington, DC 20036
202-331-1380

**National Education Association (NEA)**
1201 16th Street NW
Washington, DC 20036
202-833-4000

**National Information Center for Children and Youth with Disabilities**
P.O. Box 1492
Washington, D.C. 20013

**National Youth Sports Foundation**
10 Meredith Circle
Department P
Needham, Mass. 02192
For information about providing for the well being of children participating in sports, send a self addressed, stamped envelope.

**U.S. General Services Administration Consumer Information Center**
P.O. Box 100
Pueblo, CO 81002
Write for a list of hundreds of publications on a wide variety of topics.

**The Orton Dyslexia Society**
724 York Road
Baltimore, MD 21204
Send $3 postpaid to receive several brochures, including a list of helpful publications.

# APPENDIX B

# FOR FURTHER READING

*Nothing But the Best: Making Day Care Work For You and Your Child* by Diane Lusk (William Morrow)

*Is This Your Child?* by Doris Rapp (Quill, William Morrow, New York, 1991) This book shows parents how to identify the common foods, chemicals, or common allergic substances that could be the culprits that cause some children or adults to feel cranky, aggressive, hyperactive, unwell, depressed, or for those who are slow learners.

*Dare To Discipline* by Dr. James Dobson (Tyndale House)

*Games For Learning* by Peggy Kaye (The Noonday Press)

*The Preschool Years* by Ellen Galinsky and Judy David (Ballantine)

*What Your 1st Grader Needs To Know* by E.D. Hirsch Jr. (Doubleday)

*Making Schools Better: How Parents and Teachers Across the Country Are Taking Action— And How You Can, Too* by Larry Martz (Times Books/Random House)

*Mothers Talk About Learning Disabilities* by Elizabeth Weiss (Prentice Hall)

*More Everyday Parenting: The Six-to-Nine-Year-Old* by Robin Goldstein (Penguin Books)

*The National PTA Talks To Parents: How to Get the Best Education for Your Child* by Melitta J. Cutright (Doubleday)

*Megaskills: How Families Help Children Succeed in Schools and Beyond* by Dorothy Rich (Houghton Mifflin)

# APPENDIX C

# CATALOGS

For busy people, or those who do not live in a metropolitan area, mail order catalogs are a time saving way to shop, and can give you easy access to that hard to find toy.

## Children's Catalogs

These catalogs offer a variety of toys, puzzles, games, and outdoor equipment. Some also have selected books, videos and audios.

| | |
|---|---|
| Back to Basics Toys | (800) 356-5360 |
| Childcraft | (800) 631-5657 |
| Constructive Playthings | (800) 832-0572 |
| FAO Schwarz | (800) 426-8097 |
| Great Kids Company | (800) 533-2166 |
| Hand in Hand | (800) 872-9745 |
| HearthSong | (800) 325-2502 |
| One Step Ahead | (800) 274-8440 |
| Reader's Digest Kids | (800) 458-3014 |
| Right Start Catalog | (800) 548-8531 |
| Sensational Beginnings | (800) 444-2147 |
| Toys to Grow On | (800) 542-8338 |

## School Catalogs of Interest

| | |
|---|---|
| Community Playthings | (800) 777-4244 |
| Environments | (800) 342-4453 |
| Learning Resources | (800) 222-3909 |

## Specialty Catalogs

| | |
|---|---|
| Chinaberry (books) | (800) 776-2242 |
| Educational Insights | (800) 933-3277 |
| Lego Shop At Home | (203) 763-4011 |
| National Geographic | (800) 638-4077 |
| Nature Company | (800) 227-1114 |
| Pleasant Company (dolls) | (800) 845-0005 |
| T.C. Timbers (wooden toys) | (800) 359-1233 |

# Audio and Visual Catalogs

| | |
|---|---|
| Alacazar's Records and Kids World of Music | (800) 541-9904 |
| Coalition for Quality Children's Videos | (800) 331-6197 |
| Video Opera | (800) 262-8600 |
| Music For Little People | (800) 727-2233 |
| Signals WGBH Educational Foundation | (800) 669-9696 |
| Wireless | (800) 669-9999 |

# APPENDIX D

# PUBLICATIONS OF INTEREST

The following helpful booklets are available free from the American Academy of Pediatrics.

"You and Your Pediatrician: Common Childhood Problems"

"Your Child's Growth: Developmental Milestones"

"Surviving Coping with Adolescent Depression and Suicide"

"Television and the Family"

"Sports and Your Child"

"Alcohol: Your Child and Drugs"

"Marijuana: Your Child and Drugs"

"Cocaine: Your Child and Drugs"

Send a separate self-addressed, stamped, business sized envelope for each brochure to:

Brochure Name
Department C
American Academy of Pediatrics
P.O. Box 927
Elk Grove Village, IL 60009-0927

The **Parent Information Center** provides information, support, training, and consultation to parents of children with disabilities. They have a library of publications that can be ordered. Write to:

P.O. Box 1422
Concord, NH 03302
(603) 224-7005

The **American Reading Council** has prepared a series of manuals to help parents encourage their children to become readers. Include the ages of your children and $2.50 for postage and handling when requesting materials. Ask for "Help Your Child At Home to Become A Reader." Write to:

The American Reading Council
45 John Street, Suite 811
New York, New York 10038

# APPENDIX E

# MAGAZINES FOR CHILDREN

When choosing a magazine for your child, ask yourself these questions:
- Is the magazine right for my child's age and interests?
- Does it have an appealing format and design?
- Is the quality worth the price?

*Boodle: By Kids For Kids* (ages 6–12)
P.O. Box 1049
Portland, IN 47371
Four issues per year chockful of original poems, stories and art by children.

*Child Life* (ages 7–9)
P.O. Box 567
1110 Waterway Boulevard
Indianapolis, IN 46206

*Chickadee* (ages 3–7)
Young Naturalist Foundation
56 The Esplanade
Suite 306
Toronto, Ontario M5E 1A7, Canada
(416) 868-6001
A science and nature magazine intended to interest children in their environment and the world around them. Stories, crafts, puzzles, science experiments, and articles on animals and nature.

*Cricket* (ages 6–12)
Open Court Publishing Company
1058 Eighth Street
La Salle, IL 61301
A literary magazine with literature, nature, science, history, astronomy, art, music, sports, crafts, cartoons, and puzzles. Intended to create a love of reading, appreciation for good writing and illustration and an understanding of cultural values of all people.

*Games Junior* (ages 6–12)
P.O. Box 2082
Harlan, IA 51593
A rich variety of challenging word, picture, logic and number puzzlers. Six issues a year.

*Hidden Pictures* (ages 6–10)
P.O. Box 53781
Boulder, CO 80322
Crosswords, mazes, and hidden pictures to ponder from the editors of *Highlights.* Six issues a year.

*Highlights for Children* (ages 2–12)
2300 West Fifth Avenue
Columbus, Ohio 43216
A general interest magazine with original stories, articles, hidden pictures, activities, and puzzles. Designed to help children grow in basic skills, knowledge, creativity, sensitivity to others, and the ability to think and reason.

*Humpty Dumpty's Magazine* (ages 4–6; excellent for beginning readers)
P.O. Box 567
1110 Waterway Boulevard
Indianapolis, IN 46206

*Jack and Jill* (ages 6–8)
P.O. Box 567
1110 Waterway Boulevard
Indianapolis, IN 46206

*Kids by Kids for Kids* (ages 5–15; written by children)
Kids' Publishers, Inc.
777 Third Avenue
New York, NY 10017

*Ladybug* (ages 4–9)
Cricket Country Lane
Box 50284
Boulder, CO 80321-0284
(800) 284-7257 ext. 4L
A collection of stories, games, and educational activities aimed at creating a love of reading, developing imagination and sensibilities, and encouraging read-aloud sessions in families.

*National Geographic World*
P.O. Box 2330
Washington, DC 20077-9955
A full color magazine designed to improve geographic information, to open windows to the world, and to stimulate creative thinking and activity. Outdoor adventure, natural history, science, astronomy, social science, sports, games, crafts, and puzzles.

*Odyssey* (ages 6–12)
Cobblestone Publishing Inc.
30 Grove Street
Peterborough, NH 03458
A black and white and full color astronomy magazine designed to spark interest in

space exploration. Each issue focuses on a specific theme. Original articles on space, astronomy, NASA, observatories, and a robot named Ulysses 4-11.

*Ranger Rick* (ages 6–12)
National Wildlife Federation
8925 Leesburg Pike
Vienna, VA 22184
A natural history magazine devoted to inspiring an understanding and appreciation of the natural world and environmental issues. Filled with lots of beautiful pictures of animals. Also nature, science, astronomy, and activities.

*Sesame Street Magazine* (for preschool children, includes parent's guide)
Children's Television Workshop Inc.
North Road
Poughkeepsie, NY 12601
A general interest magazine designed to educate and entertain while helping preschoolers make the transition from television to printed material. Activities, articles and stories on people from many cultures and careers.

*Spark* (ages 5–12, some activities for preschoolers also)
P.O. Box 5027
Harlan, IA 51593-2527
Features 9 issues with great activities for kids as well as art history, writing ideas and a parents' pull-out section, with activities for preschoolers too.

*Sports Illustrated for Kids* (ages 6–12)
P.O. Box 830607
Birmingham, AL 35283-0607

*Stone Soup* (ages 6–12)
P.O. Box 83
Santa Cruz, CA 95063
For aspiring young writers, this magazine publishes original stories, poems, and art by children. Six issues per year.

*Your Big Backyard* (for preschool children and their parents)
National Wildlife Federation (800) 432-6564
Helps introduce preschoolers to nature using big colorful pictures, short features, and simple activities.

# APPENDIX F

# SPECIALIST IN ENVIRONMENTAL MEDICINE

As mentioned in Chapter 14, if you suspect your child has an allergy, environmental or food sensitivity, you can write to the following to find the nearest well trained ecologic physician. As with all medical specialists, each member practices in a somewhat individualized manner and some may be preferable to others because of your particular needs. They all however share one basic concept, namely they attempt to find the specific cause of each individual's particular illness and eliminate it if at all possible.

*Environmental medicine or clinical ecology:*

**American Academy of Environmental Medicine**
P.O. Box 16106
Denver, Colorado 80216

*Ear Specialists (otolaryngologists):*

**American Academy of Otolaryngic Allergy**
Suite 302
1101 Vermont Avenue, N.W.
Washington, D.C. 20005

*Various specialists who incorporate allergy in their practices:*

**Pan-American Allergy Society**
P.O. Box 947
Fredericksburg, Texas 78624

# APPENDIX G

# DRUG EDUCATION AND TREATMENT

**American Council for Drug Education**
204 Monroe Street, Suite 110
Rockville, MD 20850
(301) 294-0600
Offers nearly 60 publications about drugs and drug use, on such topics as prevention, warning signs, and health risks. ACDE's literature tends to be heavy on the facts but it is full of worthwhile information.

**Beginning Alcohol and Addictions Basic Education Studies (BABES)**
17330 Northland Park Court
Southfield, MI 48075
(800) 54-BABES
Produces information packets for parents, teachers, and school administrators, designed to help them keep children away from drugs.

**National Clearinghouse for Alcohol and Drug Information**
P.O. Box 2345
Rockville, MD 20852
(301) 468-2600
NCADI may be a parent's best bet: The agency provides a wealth of free information and referrals. Ask for their 35-page catalog, which lists all the articles and pamphlets available.

**The National Drug Information Center of Families in Action**
2296 Henderson Mill Road, Suite 204
Atlanta, GA 30345
(404) 934-6364
Serves as the epicenter for a nationwide network of parent groups and can refer you to a program in your area. Publishes a quarterly drug abuse update for $25 a year.

**National Prevention Network**
444 North Capitol, Suite 520
Washington, DC 20001
(202) 783-6868
Puts callers in touch with their state prevention coordinators, who have information about local drug-abuse prevention programs.

*Treatment*

**The National Institute on Drug Abuse Hotline**
(800) 662-HELP
Provides referrals for treatment across the nation.

217

**The Psychiatric Institutes of America's Hotline**
(800) COCAINE
Refers callers to treatment centers and support groups in their area. Be sure to ask whether programs are public or private, as the hotline recommends both.

# APPENDIX H

# A PARENT'S AND TEACHER'S GUIDE TO THE U.S. DEPARTMENT OF EDUCATION

**1-800-USA-LEARN Telephone Bank**

The Information Resource Center (IRC) is the public service component of the GOALS 2000 project, which supports grassroots, community-wide efforts to reach the National Education Goals. The IRC provides information about resources, Department publications, and upcoming events, including the monthly Satellite Town Meeting. Free publications include topics on early childhood education, higher education, drug prevention, technology, and a community newsletter.

**OERI Information Office**

The Office of Educational Research and Improvement maintains a toll-free telephone line staffed by trained information specialists who field more than 40,000 requests a year for information and publications. Call for information about education statistics, educational research information and publications published by OERI. The number is **1-800-424-1616** or **202-219-1513** within the Washington, D.C. metropolitan area.

**Financial Aid Information**

The Department of Education provides information about how to apply for Student Financial Aid. Call **1-800-433-3243**

**Office of the Inspector General**

The office of the Inspector General provides a hotline for individuals to call to report instances of fraud, waste or abuse involving the Department of Education funds or programs. Anyone having such knowledge should call **1-800-MIS-USED.** All callers can be assured of absolute confidentiality.

# BIBLIOGRAPHY

Ames, Louise Bates; Gillespie, Clyde; Haines, Jacqueline; Ilg, Frances L.: *The Gesell Institute's Child from One to Six: Evaluating the Behavior of the Preschool Child.* New York, Harper & Row, 1979.

Balaban, Nancy: Get closer to your child's caregiver. *Working Mother Magazine,* August 1991.

Bercow, Larry: Phone pages. *Parents Magazine,* January 1990.

Berman, Eleanor: Teaching your child self-control. *Working Mother Magazine,* August 1991.

Biehler, Robert F.: *Child Development: An Introduction.* Boston, Houghton Mifflin, 1976.

Bjorklund, David and Barbara: A clearer view of television. *Parents Magazine,* November, 1989.

Bounds, Mary C.: You can find the right preschool. *Parenting,* September 1993.

Bradley, Buff: How to raise smart kids. *Parenting,* September 1993.

Calvert, Catherine: The teacher is there to help. *Sesame Street Parent's Guide,* September 1993.

Cullinan, Bernice E.: *Read To Me: Raising Kids Who Love To Read.* New York, Scholastic, 1992.

Dobson, Dr. James: *Dare to Discipline.* New York, Bantam, 1970.

Elder, Janet: Smart talk about gifted children. *Child Magazine,* September 1990.

Francis, Roberts: Rumors of a bad teacher. *Parents Magazine,* January 1989. Does phonics cure reading problems? January 1989. How to complain. January 1990. Historic Places. August 1990. Parents as partners. September 1990. Whole language learning. September 1990.

Friedman, Jenny: Helping your learning disabled child. *Parents Magazine,* December 1989.

Galinsky, Ellen; David, Judy: *The Preschool Years — Family Strategies That Work from Experts and Parents.* New York, Ballantine, 1988.

Green, Diana Huss: *Parents' Choice.* Kansas City, Andrews and McMeel, 1993.

Hoag, Doane R.: *Genius Grew Up to Squander Talents as Adding Machine Clerk.* Atlanta Constitution, copyright 1978.

Honig, Alice S.: *Playtime Learning Games For Young Children.* Syracuse, Syracuse University Press, 1982.

Hopkins, Ellen: What kids really learn in sex-ed. *Parents Magazine,* September 1993.

Jersild, Arthur T.; Telford, Charles W.; Sawrey, James M.: *Child Psychology.* Seventh edition. Englewood Cliffs, Prentice-Hall, 1975.

Jones, Claudia: *Parents are Teachers Too.* Charlotte, Williamson, 1988.

Katz, Debra Morgenstern: Tie my shoe. *Parents Magazine,* September 1993.

Katz, Lilian: Monitoring TV time. *Parents Magazine,* January 1989.

Maeroff, Gene: The measure of a good school. *Parenting,* May 1989

Maynard, Joyce: Phonic boom. *Parenting,* September 1993.

Morrison, George S.: *Early Childhood Education Today.* Third edition. Columbus, Charles E. Merrill, 1984.

Oppenheim, Joanne; Oppenheim, Stephanie: *The Best Toys, Books and Videos for Kids.* New York, Harper Perennial, 1993.

Piaget, Jean: *Genetic Epistemology.* New York, Columbia Press, 1970.

Rotaryanns of Marietta Rotary Club: *Rotary Recipes To Remember.* Atlanta, Peachtree Printing, 1974.

Schulman, Michael: Great minds start with great questions. *Parents Magazine,* September 1993.

Schwager, Dr. Istar: What did you do in school today? *Sesame Street Parents Guide,* September 1993.

Schwartzberg, Neala: Of two minds. *Child Magazine,* September 1990.

Segell, Michael: What you should know about preschool testing. *Parents Magazine,* October 1990.

Shuker-Haines, Franny: The child guide to manic mornings. *Child Magazine,* September 1990.

Towle, Lisa: How to teach school bus safety. *Parents Magazine,* September 1990.

Weiss, Jiri: Smart computer programs for kids. *Parenting,* September 1993.

Williams, Juan: Drug prevention, never too young. *Parenting,* May 1989.

Van Til, William: *Education: A Beginning,* Second Edition. Boston, Houghton Mifflin, 1974.

# INDEX